THE PATIENT WILL SEE YOU NOW

WHY VISIBILITY, PATIENT EXPERIENCE, AND DIGITAL MARKETING IS THE KEY TO HELPING MEDICAL PRACTICES THRIVE

CRAWFORD IFLAND

MESSENGER

Published by Messenger.

ISBN 978-1-7325857-2-0 (eBook Edition)

ISBN 978-1-7325857-3-7 (Paperback Edition)

Printed and bound in the United States of America

First printing August 2018

For more practice marketing resources and articles, visit **www.messenger.md**

CONTENTS

PREFACE

The amount of information our society produces and consumes on a daily basis is staggering. In 2011, Americans took in five times the amount of information as they did in 1986 – the equivalent of 175 newspapers a day. During our leisure time (not counting time at work), each of us processes an average of 34 gigabytes (or 100,000 words) per day. Five exabytes (5 x 10^18 bytes) of new information was produced in January 2012 alone – that's more than 50,000 times the number of *words* in the entire Library of Congress.

We've created a world with 300 exabytes (that's 300,000,000,000,000,000,000 pieces) of human-made information, and this information is growing each and every second of the day. If each of these pieces of information were written on a 3x5 index card, just *one person's share* of this information would cover every square inch of Massachusetts and Connecticut combined.

It's clear that we're drowning in a sea of information. But if you want to stand out as a medical practice in such a noisy world, where should you turn? How can you thrive?

Increasingly, the ability of an medical practice to thrive is dependent on how *visible* they are – on how well they are seen and perceived by their patients. Quality of care still matters – and it always will – but more and more, the *experience* patients have at a medical practice is dictating how well that practice will do in the future. We've all heard the phrase "the doctor will see you now." But in our ever-changing world of endless information and increased patient choice, a more apt phrase might be "the *patient* will see you now."

The visibility of your practice and the experience you deliver across all aspects of your brand is a major factor in how well you will perform. If you want your practice to thrive in this sea of information, you must stand out and tell a story that is unique and appealing to potential patients.

And in our information age, it all starts with your digital marketing.

About Us

The book you're holding in your hands is the result of many years' experience in marketing for the medical industry. Messenger, the creative agency I run and the publisher of this book, is an experienced marketing agency specializing in custom medical website design, Search Engine Optimization, practice promotional videos, and more.

Patient experience is at the heart of everything we do. We exist to help physicians improve patient experience online and through their practices as well. Throughout the years, we have worked with some of the nation's leading physicians and medical technology companies to help refine their brands and grow their practices through web design, promotional videos, and marketing materials. We've helped cataract and refractive practices, medical device companies, aesthetics practices, and biotech firms grow their businesses by bridging the gap between themselves and their patients.

We utilize a smart mix of medical website design, search engine optimization, internet marketing and paid advertising, social media marketing and management, web analytics, video/audio production, and much more. We don't believe in one-size-fits-all solutions or cookie-cutter approaches to digital marketing: every practice is unique, and their online marketing should reflect that. Bottom line? We exist to help and serve physicians and their patients, not the other way around.

Through this book we hope to share some of what we've learned so that you can apply these techniques and improve your practice marketing as well.

How to Use this Book

This book is laid out into 3 sections about digital marketing:

I. *Your Website: A Key Part of Patient Experience*
II. *Gaining Visibility Through Search Engine Optimization*
III. *Engaging Patients Everywhere on the Internet*

The chapters in each section will explore various topics, including website design, video resources, SEO best practices for physicians, social media, and more. Undergirding each topic in this book is the common theme of delivering an exceptional experience to your patients. A good experience with your practice is a major reason your patients will remember you and sing your praises.

Each chapter will contain recommendations and resources we suggest you utilize to make the most of your practice marketing. These recommendations are compiled from common issues our typical clients encounter; however, each medical practice is unique and your needs may vary. While we don't believe in cookie-cutter solutions, the tools and tips we suggest in each chapter have been tested and proven to both help *patients* find what they're looking for and help *physicians* make better decisions which deliver better online experiences.

One item of note before we dive in: this book only explores topics related to *organic* marketing – topics that don't require an advertising budget. Search Engine Marketing and paid advertising on search and social platforms are entirely different subjects, ones about which we could write a separate book. While paid advertising is a very important component of any practice marketing plan, we won't address it here. In this book, we'll focus only on the strategies and tactics you can use to attract more patients that *don't* require any paid advertising.

OTHER RESOURCES

As a companion resource to this book, we have created a **90-Day Digital Marketing Action Plan** to help you take what you've learned and apply it to your medical practice. You may want to go through the Action Plan yourself, or you may want to hand it off to the person responsible for your website and marketing at your practice. Regardless of *who* does the work, we hope that it is helpful in your quest to take your website and digital marketing – and ultimately, your patient experience – to the next level.

To access the Action Plan,
visit **www.messenger.md/action-plan**

For individualized recommendations on how your practice can improve in its digital marketing, contact us at
www.messenger.md/contact

PART I

YOUR WEBSITE: A KEY PART OF PATIENT EXPERIENCE

1

YOUR WEBSITE IS THE LIFEBLOOD OF YOUR PRACTICE

What Makes a Good Physician Website?

You'd be hard-pressed to find a doctor these days who doesn't have a website. Upon further inspection, however, you might suspect that many in the medical community don't care much about their website or online reputation: their websites aren't responsive, pages are out of date, they are hard to navigate…the problems can go on and on.

Now more than ever, patients utilize the Internet to find their next practice, research their potential choices by reading reviews, and a whole host of other activities. In fact, *9 out of 10 patients will begin their search for a doctor online before they ever pick up the phone or come in for a visit.*

Everybody claims to know that a good website is an

essential element in a marketing plan that attracts new patients and fosters growth, but if you want to realize that growth for your practice, you first need to know the key elements that will make your website the most useful resource it can be.

A really great physician website is just one tool within a holistic strategy that doctors must use for patient acquisition and retention. Using best practices like responsive web design and SEO optimization can help take your website to the next level, attract new patients, and grow your practice. Let's look at some attributes of a successful physician website.

A good website helps refine your message

When you think about online marketing of your services, it's crucial to think about consistency, especially in your messaging. Many patients will come across your website while researching their options for surgery or other medical procedures, a process that can be time-consuming and overwhelming to the Average Joe. When you clearly, consistently communicate your practice's expertise and services across each digital marketing channel you employ (especially your website), you can help the patient in their decision process, making their life easier.

Using strategic content marketing and design, your website will demonstrate the knowledge and expertise you possess while highlighting what the practice does best and why the patient should select you for their medical needs. If there are any inconsistencies in your messaging, your product offerings, or your expertise, patients can easily get scared away, which costs you business and can even hurt your reputation.

A good website should attract more patients

The medical field is often new and intimidating to many patients, and your website will be the first place most of your patients will land. A strong, informative website is essentially the practice's calling card, as it is able to concisely demonstrate the full breadth of knowledge and expertise you possess. A website that is useful to patients should help them understand their condition and their options.

Aside from word-of-mouth referrals, your website is one of the strongest ways to attract new patients, many of whom are now accustomed to doing extensive internet research on potential physicians. Research has shown that it takes people an average of seven "touch points" with your brand before they will come to be familiar with your brand and begin to trust it, so repeated exposure is key.

Good web design signals to prospective patients that the practice is serious about giving their patients the best experience. In fact, if a website isn't mobile-responsive or well laid-out, the vast majority of visitors take that as an indication that the company doesn't care.

In addition to being a calling card, a good website is also indicative of how well practices are able to adopt and adapt to new technologies. While subtle, this signals to the patient that the practice has taken the time to understand the patient and ensure that they are taken care of at every level. After all, if a practice isn't investing in their public image through their website and digital marketing, how can the patient be assured that the practice has adequately invested in technologies necessary for patient care and other non-public aspects of their practice?

A good website can dramatically help with SEO

Search Engine Optimization has become ubiquitous in this day and age, and it still reigns supreme for businesses in every sector. One of the key ways patients find new doctors is through search engines: according to a 2013 study conducted by Pew Research, when asked to think about the last time they hunted for health or medical information 77% of online health seekers say they began at a search engine such as Google, Bing, or Yahoo – and these numbers have only grown in recent years.

This demonstrates just how important SEO is for successful internet marketing. Re-designing your practice website (and regularly updating it) can signal to Google that you have invested significant time and attention to your website, leading their robots to more frequently index your site.

If done correctly, your website should show up higher in

search engine rankings. Regardless of whether you completely re-design your website or just make some adjustments, following SEO best practices and making sure each page is optimized for Google and other search engines can be a boon for your business. We'll cover this topic more in our section about SEO, but for now, know that a good SEO strategy is one of the major pillars in a successful, holistic practice marketing plan.

A good website can lend your practice personality

Both new and existing patients want to feel like their medical provider has a distinct "personality" and is a welcoming place. We've seen a ton of practice websites that are old, out-of-date, or don't accurately reflect the practice's current offerings and expertise. Updating your website to convey not only what you do but *why* you do it can be incredibly beneficial in fostering patient trust.

Creating a safe space where patients can learn about your practice, the people behind it, and directly interact with you is a great strategy for attracting new patients and retaining prior patients. Giving your practice a personality through solid, effective web design demonstrates that patients will get the care and attention they deserve rather than feeling like yet another face in the crowd.

A good website should also differentiate your practice from your competitors. Chances are your market is crowded.

Having a good website will give you a competitive advantage over those competitors who haven't paid close attention to their online reputation. This means not only having a well-designed website but making sure you're showing up at the top of search engine results so that when patients search for doctors in their area, they find you.

A good website can make your staff more efficient

If done correctly, a new website is also a fantastic tool to create and improve internal efficiency. Tools and pages such as FAQs, appointment requests, click-to-call functionality, live chat, and downloadable patient forms can help save your patient – and your practice staff – valuable time.

Not only will it save time, but it can help lead to happier patients and staff, too. With such tools available to them, patients are able to quickly access information, fill out forms ahead of time and submit questions directly through the site rather than calling the office. This means your staff can have more time on their hands to deal with business issues rather than answering the same patient question dozens of times every day.

A good website promotes a coherent brand.

If you want to stand out in a crowded market, you need to have a brand that is clear, coherent, and cohesive across all platforms.

Ideally, your website will bring all elements of your brand – your physical presence, your social media, your paid advertising, and your content marketing – under one roof and help tell a coherent story. Patients resonate with clear and authentic stories, so utilizing your website as a platform to tell your story will elevate your brand in the minds of your patients.

A GOOD WEBSITE IS FLEXIBLE.

Technology is constantly changing, and your website is no exception. A good practice website should remain relevant and up-to-date with the latest technological advances, giving you an advantage over practices whose websites aren't well-maintained.

Having a website that works on a variety of devices, is easy-to-navigate, and is flexible to the needs of the patient will go a long way in helping to win the trust of your patients. We'll get into this topic more in our chapter on responsive web design, but for now, just know that if your website doesn't look good on mobile devices, you'll be losing out on many potential patients.

A GOOD WEBSITE WILL CONTAIN VALUABLE CONTENT – AND LOTS OF IT.

You've probably heard it said that "Content is King." There's a very good reason that statement rings true. Especially in the medical field, where patients are confronted with medical jargon, the unknown, and the prospect of surgery, the more information, the better.

Having a website that's chock-full of content and information to set patients' minds at ease is a must. Educational blog posts and video resources are a great way to educate patients about their options, including surgical procedures. We'll explore this topic more in our chapter on content marketing, but every physician website should have lots of valuable content for their patients to discover and engage with the practice.

A GOOD WEBSITE FACILITATES CONVERSATION.

What good is a website if patients can't contact you for more information? *Lack of easy-to-find contact information is one of the biggest reasons patients abandon websites without ever scheduling an appointment or requesting more information.* A practice website that helps you grow will provide patients multiple opportunities to contact the practice for more information or to schedule an appointment. Having clear, easy-to-find contact information on every page of your website is key.

Common Mistakes Physicians Make with Their Websites

It's unlikely that you studied website design in medical school, and if you're trying to do it yourself, chances are you're struggling to keep your head above water. Even if you have someone on your team managing your website and online marketing, they most likely have other projects on their plate as well, so your website may fall to the back burner.

If you're worried that your website might not be measuring up, here are some signs your practice might need help with web design.

Your website isn't mobile-responsive

With an ever-increasing number of prospective patients turning to mobile devices to conduct quick searches, it's critical that your website is mobile responsive. In fact, Google has admitted that over 50% of searches on its platform are conducted on mobile devices. If your website is not responsive, not only will patients have a hard time finding the information they're looking for, but Google and other search engines are more likely to penalize your site with lower search rankings.

You're not clear on the basics of SEO

The purpose of your website is to attract prospective patients to your practice, but if they can't find you in the first place it won't do you any good. That's where Search Engine Optimization (SEO) comes in. SEO best practices ensure that both Google and patients will have the best chance possible of locating your practice when they're searching for the products and services that you offer.

You don't have lead generation forms to help you gather information from prospective patients

Collecting data is crucial for allowing you to stay in touch with potential patients. It will also allow you to grow that potential client base over time by offering valuable resources and materials that are more likely to turn them into paying patients. Your website is the perfect tool for this – consider implementing lead generation forms that collect basic patient information (like a name and an email address) to grow your subscriber base.

Your website isn't increasing your conversion rates...

Your website should be bringing patients into your practice. If you don't have a tool in place for tracking conversion rates, you'll have no idea whether or not you are effectively reaching your target audience and getting them to take desired actions. Consider working with someone who can create, maintain, and improve upon lead generation funnels to increase conversion rates.

...or, you don't know how to interpret your analytics at all.

Chances are you have basic reporting and analytics tools available on your website, but if you don't know how to interpret the data, it won't be very useful to you. What's a bounce rate, you ask? Is a 2% CTR good, bad, or horrible? Having someone on your team who can help you interpret what your website visitors are doing is essential.

YOUR WEBSITE ISN'T ADEQUATELY SERVING YOUR CURRENT PATIENTS.

Your website isn't just a tool for attracting new patients – it's also an excellent tool for nurturing existing patient relationships. Tools like patient portals, information about surgical complications, and additional resources should be available to help take your existing patient relationships to the next level.

How to Build a Website Which Will Benefit Your Practice

If you're planning to build a new website (or redesign an existing one) for your practice, you need to begin by understanding a somewhat inconvenient truth: *most websites don't work very well.*

Marketing company HubSpot submitted more than a million websites to an automated website grading tool, measuring the effectiveness of each in four key categories. The average score for mobile optimization was a D, for SEO, a D–; for Performance, a D–, and for Security, an F. The overall average score was a 59 – *a failing grade.*

If that data seems a little obscure, consider your own experience online. How many websites have you visited that didn't work on your smartphone or tablet? How many looked just like dozens of other sites you've seen? How many focused more on the company than on you, the consumer? How many made it hard to find the information you were looking for?

There are two keys to smart medical website design. The first key is to *have a clear set of goals:* what, in other words, do you want your website to do for your practice? For example, do you want to attract site visitors and convert them into new patients, or help current patients schedule appointments online? Do you want the ability to make changes on your site yourself, without the help of a web designer? Do you want the ability to see metrics on visitors and visitor behavior on your site?

The second key is to *match the design of your website to those goals.* If one of the goals of your website is to grow your practice, the first thing you should realize is this: prospective patients need to find it. When they do find your practice, you need to achieve a variety of things, including:

1. Differentiating yourself from other practices;
2. Providing site visitors with helpful information;
3. Making it easy for them to navigate to the information they want; and
4. Continually updating your site with fresh content so repeat visitors view your practice as thriving and growing.

A Guide to Choosing the Best Web Design Agency for Your Practice

When it comes to designing your website, you have many options. Some people choose to design their website themselves, but for many, the complexity of designing the site and learning the technology required to make the website actually work is too much – they'd rather hire someone with design expertise to do it for them. If that's you, don't worry – you're not alone.

Individuals and businesses hire design agencies all the time for a variety of different reasons. Some people may have the technical expertise, but not the time. Others may have the time, but the process of creating a functional website is over their head. That's where a designer or design agency comes in.

But before you hire someone to design and develop your practice website, it's important to know the different types of designers, what you can expect from each, and how to make the process the very best it can be. There's a design agency to fit everyone's needs. To find the best one for you, let's explore a few different types of website designers.

The Generalist

The Generalist is a solo designer or small design agency who will build a website for absolutely anybody. If you can fog a mirror, they can build you a website!

- **What they say:** "We offer full-service custom website development plans designed for small businesses, freelance professionals, and non-profit organizations."
- **What they mean:** "We claim that we have expertise in every category known to man, but we really just have a few templates with different stock photos and contact information. We're not really that concerned about quality, and your website will look the same as everyone else's. It doesn't matter to us if you're multi-million dollar law firm in Manhattan or a local Boy Scout Troop – just give us your $799 one-time fee and leave us alone."
- **How they do it:** Templates and volume. The Generalist will pay thousands of dollars in Google PPC ads per month just to earn your click. They'll lure you in with a low, one-time fee of $799 to build your website. They'll obtain your content from your current website and have an army of freelancers overseas copy and paste your text, slap a few stock photos on it, and call it "custom." A complete website will take them a day or two to make and cost them maybe $100 in labor. Oh, and don't forget the hidden hosting fees, change fees, and lengthy contracts that tie you down to them and nobody else. Multiply a $799 profit per site by a few hundred websites per year, and you've got yourself a profitable business.

- **What you'll get:** Technically, you'll get a website. It may or may not be responsive, and it will almost definitely look like others on the web. It likely won't utilize a content management system, which means that future content additions or changes will be costly and have to be hard-coded in by someone on the other side of the world. Your website likely won't be optimized for SEO, and if anything breaks, you're on the hook for expensive changes and fees for everything.

The Big Company

- **What they say:** "We are an experienced digital medical marketing agency utilizing a wide array of talent to achieve our customers goals. We combine programmers, designers, marketers, copywriters, strategists, consultants, and IT professionals to provide a high quality digital marketing experience for our customers."
- **What they mean:** "We've been at this for a long time. We do specialize in one industry and claim to make truly unique services to our clients, but if we're being honest, we have a few templates and still farm the majority of our work out to India. It's only because we have lots of clients in this one industry that we appear to be unique."
- **How they do it:** Most of their employees will be

focused in sales and support. They'll have a US-based office, but most of the actual work will be done in Southeast Asia. The Big Company will take more time to discover what content is meaningful to you and create a site that attempts to fit your needs (rather than the Generalist's approach of forcing you into a 5-page template), but at the end of the day, most of their development will take place overseas, utilizing templates that appear to be more unique.

- **What you'll get:** You'll get a website that appears more unique than one made by The Generalist, but if you do enough searching you'll discover that most websites The Big Company builds may not look exactly the same – but they are very similar. They'll all have the same functionality, and don't expect great quality photos – they'll be stock photos marked up by The Big Company. You website may have a Content Management System attached, but The Big Company's contract will likely have you paying a hefty monthly fee for edits and changes, which you'll be tied to for a long time. While better than a website built by The Generalist, the Big Company is in the business of volume and churning through clients.

The Freelancer

- **What they say:** "I'm a designer and developer who utilizes the latest technology to craft meaningful brands and digital products. I'm dedicated to providing clients with the best experience possible."
- **What they mean:** "I've got to pay rent this month. Your site is one of many projects for me right now, and Client X is being a little more needy right now, so I'll get back to you when I can…"
- **How they do it:** Working from home and coffee shops are the name of The Freelancer's game. This isn't necessarily a bad thing, but it can mean a lack of consistency during your website design experience. The Freelancer is often juggling more than one project at once, which means there can be delays and inconsistent communication during your website design process. They'll often use the latest technology to ensure you get the best website possible, but this can mean bloated budgets if they're working hourly.
- **What you'll get:** Individual results may vary. There are tons of experienced, professional, and talented freelancers out there, but when you're hiring, you have to be selective. Many freelancers won't specialize in an industry, but a skill…so while they may be great at building websites, they may not understand the individual needs of your practice. In addition, The Freelancer's hours may be odd,

and a lack of a dedicated office may mean that their availability for a conference call or a design sprint may be limited. If you want to get the most bang for your buck, The Freelancer can be a good choice – but be sure you establish ground rules up-front and clearly communicate expectations. Don't get us wrong – freelancers can be a great way to get an incredible digital product at a fraction of the price of a larger agency with higher overhead…but you have to do your homework. Look for someone with experience in your industry who has a proven track record of satisfied clients, a good body of work, and a deep investment in the client relationship. You want someone who has been down this road before managing projects for clients like you, not someone who is just freelancing on the side for a little extra cash.

The Specialized Agency

- **What they say:** "We are a design & development firm helping organizations thrive in our digital age. We craft digital products for the human experience that help brands stand out as well as stand for something."
- **What they mean:** Often times, the Specialized Agency means exactly what it says! Their teams are experienced in building digital products for a

variety of clients (and chances are you've heard of a few of their clients before). The Agency is the team that the Big Guys use when they want to get serious about their online presence.

- **How they do it:** Everything the Specialized Agency does is custom – from websites and mobile apps to any additional functionality your digital presence needs, there's no skimping here. No templates or outsourcing here – their team will shepherd you through the design process, doing a deep dive into your practice's needs to come up with best and most innovative creative solution.
- **What you'll get:** A completely custom website from A to Z. Every aspect of your website will be designed and coded by hand and will seamlessly integrate into a content management system, eCommerce platforms (if necessary), and other web applications. You can expect more thoughtful animation and use of video throughout your site, and photography will be completely custom. In short, every piece of your website will be uniquely tailored to your needs, not the needs of somebody else. The Specialized Agency will do a deep dive to understand your needs before prescribing a "one-size-fits-all" solution.

What's Best for Your Practice?

At the end of the day, there's something for everyone. While we wouldn't necessarily recommend The Generalist, there are some individuals who need a basic website at an affordable price. Others may need something completely custom in every way, for which the Specialized Agency may be the best choice. If you're not picky about having much of a say in the design process, The Freelancer or The Big Company could be a good fit.

Your website is the lifeblood of your digital marketing – get it wrong and your practice could suffer. From SEO to video and content marketing, there are a number of ways that you can make your practice website the very best it can be, but the first – and most important – piece to get right is *how your website looks on mobile devices.* That's what we'll explore next.

2

MOBILE MATTERS: WHY YOUR PRACTICE WEBSITE NEEDS TO BE RESPONSIVE

The Unseen Risk Hiding In Your Website

When it comes to our marketing, our websites are often treated like our cars: change the oil every 3 months. Unless something breaks or a problems arises, they usually require fairly little maintenance, right? *Wrong.*

The Internet moves a little faster than the automotive industry. While a vehicle from 2007 will still drive perfectly well today, a website that hasn't been updated since then will almost certainly drive people away. There is a certain point when a website that should be an asset becomes a major liability. This can happen in many different ways, including websites that are poorly-maintained, sparsely-updated, or sites that deliver errors from a lack of proper maintenance.

But there's one particular error that often goes unnoticed when it comes to websites today – and if your website hasn't seen a massive overhaul in the past few years, there's a good possibility that it affects you. What is it, you ask?

A little thing called *responsive design.*

The Background on Responsive Design

Responsive web design is a fairly recent phenomena on the web. It became necessary with the advent of the iPhone in 2007; the smaller screen capable of displaying full web pages made a new web format necessary.

Responsive design ensures that your website looks as good on mobile devices as it does on desktops and laptops – it causes the elements on a website to rearrange *depending on the size of the screen on which they are being displayed.* With responsive design, your site will automatically conform to the dimensions of mobile devices, be easy to navigate, and make content easy to access.

Think of the content of a website like water: it adapts to fill the entire space that it is placed in. By utilizing responsive design, the end-user is afforded a much better experience. They no longer need to pinch or zoom to read text on a page, or fumble around trying to find the information they're looking for.

It has been estimated that current Internet users spend

about 2 of every 3 minutes on smartphones and tablets. Not only that, but more than 40% of Internet searches are for business purposes, so if you haven't seen a major overhaul of your website's design in recent years, chances are it's not responsive and you could be missing out on lots of potential patients.

But responsive design isn't just for users – it's good business practice as well, and is be a major contributing factor to good SEO. In fact, due to the rise in mobile traffic in recent years, Google updated their search engine algorithm in late 2017 to reward those websites that were "mobile-friendly" – and penalize those that were not.

Is My Website Responsive?

In order to help you discern whether your website is responsive or not, we've assembled a little quiz you can take at **www.messenger.md/website-quiz**

Responsive vs. Non-Responsive Websites

My Site Isn't Responsive. What Can I Do About It?

If your website is not responsive, you have a few options at your disposal. Each will be an investment, but trust us when we say that an investment in responsive web design is well worth it!

Option One: Hire a developer to retrofit your website

Media queries are little bits of code that detect the screen size of the device a website is being viewed upon and tell a browser to display elements a certain way depending on the browser's size. For instance, if a user is viewing your site on an iPhone, photos that were next to each other on a desktop computer may stack on top of each other; if you're using an iPad, they may still display the same as they do on a desktop, or they may stack like they would on mobile.

Developers can add media queries to your website fairly easily, but it takes time and effort to ensure that every element displays properly across a variety of devices. When adding media queries on an already-existing website, it is often easy for certain elements to slip through the cracks in the thousands of lines of code. *This brings us to our second option...*

Option Two: Redesign your entire website from the ground up

In terms of holistic changes designed to deliver the best experience possible, redesigning your entire website is the better of the two options, namely because it is a fresh start. While a developer can certainly add media queries to an existing website, it's all too easy for elements to go unnoticed because they aren't used very frequently. While these are minor changes to be made down the road, it means that errors and problems pop up from time to time, requiring the developer to go back in and make changes to the website (all of which costs you more time and money).

Rather than developing an ad-hoc solution, it's better to start fresh on a new design. A redesign of your practice website not only gives you an opportunity to create a new look (which can attract new users to your website), but it also can give developers a chance to go in and correct redundancies and fragmented code that has piled up over the years, factors that can lead to a faster, more reliable website and ultimately a better experience for your users.

How Patients See Your Website

While potential patients users may enter your website from a variety of different sources, there's one thing that's certain – you need them to stay. What good is your website if users only stay for a few seconds and then leave?

In order to make sure your website visitors aren't leaving quickly, you need to make a splash – and quickly. Take a look at the following stats about how much website design matters to your patients:

- 75% of users admit they decide on a company's credibility based on its website's design.
- 94% of first impressions are design-related.
- The average viewing time of your web page's main image is around 5.94 seconds.
- Users dedicate 66% of their attention to contents below the fold on a normal media page.
- 62% of companies that designed a website for mobile devices reported increased sales.

There's even more interesting information about the way patients see your website in an infographic that may be found at **www.messenger.md/website-infographic**

Need to Redesign Your Practice Website?

If you've spent more than a few years at your practice, it's likely that you've seen your website go through some changes. Sometimes they're minor – a quick addition to the staff bios, a new page here or there – but other times, the changes are far more widespread. You may change hosting services, transfer domain name providers, or update your content management system. And the largest change of all? *A complete overhaul of your practice website.*

If you're a practice administrator, head of marketing, or even a physician in your own solo practice, a website redesign can seem like a daunting task. First, you have to find a web designer who knows what they're doing. Maybe you'll go with a freelancer; maybe an agency. But will they understand the needs of your practice, or will they build a website for anybody? How much will it cost? How long will it take? What if something goes wrong? And how can you know that you're getting a good product when there are so many confusing technical terms being thrown around?

It's easy to get overwhelmed by the immense scope of a practice website redesign, especially when you're trying to manage other aspects of your business. However, every hour that your old website spends up on the Internet could mean missed opportunities, lost patients, and a brand that is diminishing in value, so it's important to navigate the redesign process efficiently. Here are some key ways you can do so.

Define what success looks like for your practice

Before you do any research on hiring a design agency, you need to define what success looks like for your practice as you embark on the journey of creating a new website.

What should the website do? What should users get out of the website, and what will the end result be for your practice? Do you want more patients? Do you want to increase the number of premium procedures you perform each year?

Asking these strategic questions and defining what success looks like for your business will help the agency you hire design a site that will achieve your business goals. After all, you're not just creating a new website to be prettier than your old one – it has to serve your business.

Develop or refine your brand strategy

Just as you wouldn't begin such a large project without thinking through how it will serve your business, you shouldn't begin without considering how it will serve your target audience. This is where your brand comes into play.

How do you want users to feel when they visit your website? And what is your target audience, after all? Are you targeting Millennials who want a premium, luxury experience with their LASIK surgery? Or is your target demographic an aging population who wants to know they're in good hands with their cataract procedure?

Defining what your brand will be (and who it will be for) is one of the most important things you can do. Before any code is written or any pages are designed, defining what your brand will be and who it will be for should be your focus.

Decide on a content strategy

One of the best ways to drive traffic to your practice website is by sharing content. Too many doctors don't understand this essential aspect of website design; instead, they adopt the "if we build it, they will come" mentality. Instead, practice marketers should use content creation as a primary means of driving traffic to your practice and establishing authority in your market. Creating useful, meaningful content means deciding on a content strategy.

For this step, you need to decide what types of content you're going to share, and how you plan on sharing them. Will your new practice website have a blog? Do you want to have a video library? Will content be freely available for anyone that wants to see it, or will it require a paid membership (or simply an email address)?

These are the questions that are important to ask (and answer) when strategizing and designing your new practice website, as they will inform layout decisions and technologies needed to make your practice website a success.

Develop a social media strategy

Content doesn't exist in a vacuum. It is created to be shared and discussed – and that's where social media comes into play. Most of us use social media, and we're familiar with the major platforms. Developing a social media strategy should be at the heart of the content strategy you developed above.

To develop a strategy, first decide where your practice should be on social media. Twitter, Facebook, and LinkedIn are all popular platforms of choice for doctors and their practices, but we've also seen some engaging examples of practices utilizing Instagram and Pinterest well.

At the end of the day, it all comes down to what you're going to post, who you're posting it for, and where you want it to be seen. *(Need some suggestions? Refer to our chapter on Social Media for the Physician).*

Measure your traffic

Creating a new practice website is a complete and total waste of time if you're not measuring traffic in order an analyze your website and see if you're meeting business objectives. Remember step #1, *Define What Success Looks Like for Your Practice*? You have to know what success looks like in real terms in order to use analytics to see if you're meeting those objectives.

But traffic, page views, and referrals aren't the whole picture – measurement also means taking into account user experience best practices, not just time spent on your site. Are users able to find the information they're looking for? Is your website usable on mobile devices, or does it become completely worthless on anything smaller than an iPad?

User interviews, surveys, and follow-ups with patients are important to understand if your new website is converting –

not just in terms of page views and vanity metrics, but also in aspects of user-friendliness, usability, and the like.

Ultimately, the determining factors in whether or not your practice website is a success are *usability* and *helpfulness*. If potential patients find your website poorly-designed or hard to use on mobile devices, you're missing out on a huge opportunity to build a trusting relationship. If user can't find what they're looking for – if your website isn't helpful in their quest to obtain information – you'll lose their interest, too.

When you take a holistic view and think about your website, content marketing, social media, and SEO strategically, a redesigned website can work wonders for your practice. It will engage more visitors, increase revenue, and help you accomplish real business goals. There are myriad resources you can make use of on your website to help you achieve these goals, but one stands out above the rest: *video.*

3

THE POWER OF VIDEO

Why Video?

"A *picture is worth a thousand words."* You've probably heard that phrase a thousand times. But according to Dr. James McQuivey, if a picture is worth 1,000 words, one minute of video is worth approximately *1.8 million.*

According to Forrester Research, video content wields an incredible power when it comes to online marketing. According to studies, the chances of getting a page one listing on Google increase 53 times with video content. Here are some more reasons why you may want to consider implementing video in your practice:

Video affects conversion rates in a big way

In order to understand the power of video as it relates to conversion rates and traditional marketing, let's take a look at the following statistics – they're quite telling of a video's power to communicate and engage:

- Video in an email results in a 200-300% increase in click-through rate.
- Including a video in a landing page can increase conversion by 80%.
- YouTube has reported that mobile video consumption increases 100% every year.
- After watching a video, users are 64% more likely to buy a product online.

If you're a physician trying to connect with executives and other industry leaders, video can be a powerful tool as well: 50% of executives look for more information after seeing a product or service in a video, and 64% of executives visit the marketer's website and 39% call a vendor after seeing a video. Video's effect on conversion rates is so powerful that 65% of marketers plan to increase their mobile ad budgets to account for video.

Video promotes and influences user interaction

Video can have some profound effects on user interaction, too. A good promotional video on a website shouldn't just be informative – it should display clear calls-to-action that enable the viewer to understand what they are to do next.

As an example of how video effects users' behavior, just look at these statistics:

- 90% of users say that product videos are helpful in the decision process.
- 92% of mobile video consumers share videos they see with others.
- One-third of all online activity is spent watching video.
- The average Internet user is exposed to an average of 32.3 videos in a month. That's at least one video per day, and this number is only expected to rise.

Not only is video a powerful tool to explain your products and services, but it has lasting effects on users' memory and retention: 80% of users recall a video advertisement that they viewed in the past 30 days.

Video is content, and "Content is King"

If you're curious about getting into online video, we should take a look at how other marketers are generating video content. Since one minute of video is supposedly worth 1.8 million words, video has great potential to increase ROI on marketing efforts. That's not because video is content – it's because it is *sticky* content, content which makes users stay longer on a web page. While good video does take more time and resources to produce, its "stickiness" is incredibly effective to encourage users to stay on your website for longer periods of time.

The most popular forms of video content are news and comedic videos, but other types of video are effective as well. In fact, so much new video is being uploaded to YouTube and other sites every day that traditional media outlets have been left in the dust: more video is uploaded to the Internet every 30 days than all three major U.S. TV networks have produced in the past 30 years.

Types of Videos for Your Medical Practice

For many patients, even the most routine medical appointment can make them nervous. Going to the doctor can be a scary prospect, even for those in apparently perfect health. Video is one of the most important – and effective – tools for physicians to use in connecting, educating, and engaging with their patients.

Not just any video will do, however. Overly complex videos with medical jargon and stats about success rates and what types of surgeries your practice performs will do nothing to draw in hesitant prospective patients. No, this is a problem of emotion: to solve it one must appeal to a patient's emotions. There are three main types of videos that physicians can use to engage more effectively with their patients.

The explainer video: seek to educate

Walking through the surgical process in exhaustive detail is a great way for people to begin understanding the process – it's a great tool to calm fears and explain how procedures and treatment work.

Once the patient knows what each step is, the surgical process is no longer a looming unknown. Instead, it becomes something that they can tackle piece by piece. There's no need to inundate the patient with overwhelming amounts of information, but in general, the more context and information you can provide, the better. Peel back the protective veil of medical jargon and explain in human terms what patients should expect from their surgery in order to empower them. Tools like Rendia are excellent ways to help educate your patients about routine procedures and set their minds at ease.

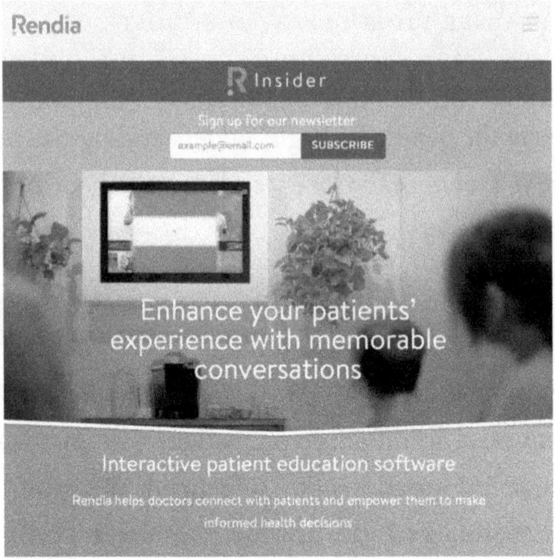

Rendia is a great tool for educational/explainer videos

The behind the scenes video: go where no patient has gone before

Perhaps one of the most effective videos a medical practice can utilize is a "behind the scenes" video. These videos are not quite as rehearsed and scripted as practice promotional videos, but they're still important tools to help patients understand more about your practice.

Behind the scenes videos often lend themselves to being shared on social media as small "glimpses" into the everyday life of your practice. Use these types of videos to help patients get to know the practice and the people in it – not just the doctors, but the back office staff who are integral parts in helping the practice run efficiently and helping patients have a terrific experience. The more patients are familiar with *all aspects* of your practice, the more comfortable they will feel when coming in for a visit or a procedure.

The promotional video: humanize to connect

Beyond seeking to educate patients, video has another powerful ability that few other forms of communication do: the ability to humanize. Putting a human face on something that's not inherently personified (a medical practice, for example) is a powerful way to help prospective patients "connect" with your practice and feel more familiar before they ever walk through the door.

Promotional video for the Eye Center of New York

Human faces build connection, authenticity, and trust – and patients will only put their health into the hands of someone they feel they can trust. Taking such a leap of faith can be hard for new patients who are unfamiliar with the process and the people behind that process, so showcasing the people behind the practice can help distinguish your practice from other providers in your market and set you apart in the minds of patients.

How to Utilize Video in Your Practice

Consider adding video patient testimonials

Traditional patient testimonials are good. *Video patient testimonials are unstoppable.*

Many physicians collect feedback and utilize patient testimonials on their practice website, and as we'll see in future chapters, this is a great strategy. While this is a good practice that offers the proven psychological factor of social proof, studies indicate that there may be an even more effective way to present that information. Just look at the statistics surrounding traditional testimonials:

- 79% of online shoppers tend to trust online reviews as much as recommendations from friends and family
- Customer reviews create a 74% increase in product conversion
- 77% of people take the time to read product/service reviews before they make an online purchase

- Customer testimonials have the highest effectiveness rating for all types of content marketing, with a rating of 89%
- 90% of consumers admit their buying decisions are influenced by online reviews

If the statistics are correct, *video testimonials* are even more powerful:

- 65% of your audience are visual learners
- Website visitors are 64% more likely to buy a product on an online retail site after watching a video
- Website visitors who view video stay on a website an average of 2 minutes longer than those who don't view videos

It's a no-brainer: video content is quite powerful. When combined with effective design, video gives potential patients and other website visitors a chance to find the information they are seeking and make an informed decision. Unlike words on a page, video offers the physician an opportunity to elicit feelings and emotion from the viewer, which can prove to be a powerful psychological marketing tool.

Consider non-traditional forms of video

If there's one big myth about video content for the

medical industry, it's that video always has to be produced and professional. Don't get us wrong – there's a big difference between a professionally-produced promotional video and a hastily-made, self-produced video shot on an iPhone, but video spans far beyond traditional applications.

Doctors can utilize the power of video to give patients "behind the scenes" glimpses into everyday life at their practice, short educational videos explaining complex surgical cases, and the like. Some surgeons have even transitioned into occasional live streaming using Facebook Live and other apps to let patients and viewers get a glimpse into the life at a medical practice – and while you'll need to be conscious of HIPAA rules and regulations, this can be a great way to show prospective patients what it's really like at your practice.

Inform, educate, and provide value

While video is an incredible marketing tool, it can also be used to make for happier patients. Video can be humorous (when appropriate), and can lead to stronger ties with patients, especially if video is used as a medium for education.

By educating your patients about their options, you are providing incredible value to them. While most patients will leave a consultation and forget much of what was said, having a video that they can refer back to is a great way to help them retain the important information you have to offer.

Because they know what to expect, educated and informed patients are far more likely to have a positive experience with their surgery, and it is less likely that they will be surprised by unforeseen complications or suboptimal surgical outcomes. While it is not possible to ensure that every patient is 100% satisfied with their results, an investment in patient education is a wise move for happier patients...and happier patients make for happier doctors.

Whatever video outlet you decide makes most sense for your practice, utilize it so that patients can connect and learn more about your story and what you have to offer. A smart video strategy can have an amazing effect on patient education, SEO, your online reputation, and referrals and new patients that discover you via video.

Practical Tips and Tricks for Implementing Video in Your Practice

Hopefully by now you can see that video is a crucial tool in any marketers' arsenal. So if you want to get started producing video content for your medical practice, here are some tips and best practices.

Keep it short

When it comes to video, you only have a limited amount of

time to capture a user's attention: only 5% of viewers will stop watching a video after 1 minute, but over 60% of viewers will stop after two minutes. Keeping a video short and incredibly informative is the number one thing that most first-time video producers get wrong. Users who are interested in learning about important things will stay longer than those hoping to be entertained, but it's still crucial to keep your videos short, sweet, and to the point.

Make it funny

Even if you're not using video as a traditional advertising strategy, it can still be powerful to make your video content engaging and enjoyable: enjoyment of video ads increase purchase intent by 97% and brand association by 139%.

There's a huge opportunity to leverage video to market your practice by creating engaging content that people actually want to see, not just creating bland, boring videos for the sake of having a video.

Be sure it loads quickly

According to Google, 4 out of 5 users will click away if the video stalls while loading. In order to ensure that your video displays quickly, be sure to compress it appropriately and upload it to a popular streaming service (such as Vimeo or Wistia) and embed it in your website rather than hosting it yourself.

Try different platforms

Regular YouTube videos are great, but don't limit yourself to video advertising or traditional videos on YouTube or Vimeo – there are lots of great ways to create fresh, engaging content for your users to view and share.

Video podcasts are another way to generate great video content, and new streaming technologies are incredible ways to show behind-the-scenes clips from your practice. Facebook Live and Instagram Stories are two new tools that marketers are using to quickly share video content that may not fit the mold of traditional video production (plus, they help with your social media content creation as well).

These new platforms are changing dynamics of how video is shared, and that's a good thing – live video shows a different side of people and businesses that users don't typically get to see in the highly-produced, "sterile" promotional videos we're all used to seeing.

Speaking of practice promotional videos, what makes one great?

What Makes an Effective Practice Promotional Video?

When it comes to digital marketing, video is king. Multiple studies have shown the impact that brand videos can make on audiences of all kinds, from increasing engagement to improving recall of your business even days after watching the video. The same is true for promotional videos for medical practices. But even though video is powerful, throwing one together isn't enough – you need to ensure that your message captivates your audience and drives them toward a consultation.

Let's take a look at the different elements that make up a great promotional video.

It captures attention immediately

Our attention span online grows shorter by the day. Statistics now place the average attention span on the Internet at 8 seconds…and if you're marketing elective services like LASIK to younger patients, it could be ever shorter than that. Any successful promotional video needs to make sure that it captures its audience's attention within these first few moments.

Don't wait to share the most compelling footage, colors, or sound. Make sure that as your audience scrolls by your video on social media or your website, they stop and pay attention (a great way to do this is with a compelling thumbnail). Get to the point quickly by illustrating the issue the viewer may be having. The best videos introduce the viewer's problem almost immediately, getting them to think, *"hey, that applies to me!"*

Sound design matters

When crafting a promotional video for your practice, make sure that your music is top-notch. Studies have long shown that music and sound can make a big difference in influencing audience behaviors; the same is true for a promotional video. Make sure that the music is interesting and engaging, but don't try to force it – having music that overpowers the voices in a video is a great way to make your viewers lose interest.

Think about color

Just like music and sound, the colors you choose for your video can have a crucial impact in how your audience subconsciously perceives your practice and its message. Yellow, for example, tends to reflect warmth and optimism, while blue conveys trust, calmness, and strength.

Colors are deeply psychological and can subliminally influence buyer behavior and feelings toward your brand, so if you're using any sort of motion graphics or animations in your video, pay attention to color. While you should always maintain brand consistency, choosing color carefully in your video marketing can have a powerful effect.

Make sure your messaging stays on topic

Attention span doesn't just matter at the beginning of your video. If your messaging ventures off-course, your potential patients may stop paying attention before you get your value proposition across. It's important to storyboard before creating a promotional video. If your goal is to get a singular message across about your medical expertise and the value of your practice, don't dilute that message to draw your audience away from that value. Instead, stay on topic for the entirety of the video, focusing your entire messaging on that singular point.

Choose authentic footage, not stock

Whenever possible, shoot authentic footage of your practice or relevant medical footage. Potential patients can spot kitschy stock video from a mile away, so try to avoid big stock companies whose libraries are filled with inauthentic corporate footage. Patients want to see the real you – even if it feels uncomfortable to be on camera, authenticity wins every time. If you need good stock footage to serve as b-roll, try a quality licensing service like Film Supply (www.filmsupply.com)

Real people foster connection

Finally, your promotional video should include people to make your brand relatable and not just an abstract concept. While explainer videos and animations are great, real people telling authentic stories capture a viewer's attention like nothing else can. That's why video is a more powerful communication medium than plain text, or even an image.

Incorporating real patients rather than just employees at your practice can help, too. Social proof has been proven to work because it allows your audience to learn about your value from someone neutral. Try to involve both your physicians, office staff, and existing patients to make sure your audience understands that your practice is making an active difference through the work you perform.

Creating great video content for your medical practice isn't easy, but it is worth it. By ensuring your video marketing contains these elements, you can take advantage of the many benefits that the video can bring you in today's digital world. Approach it strategically, and keep the above elements in mind, and your chances of attracting new patients with the power of video will increase dramatically.

But after you've created solid video content for your practice, you need to know what type of effect it is having on your practice. Have your efforts drawn in new patients? Is your content adding to the bottom line?

In order to know the effectiveness of your content, you will need to measure the results, which is why we will now turn our attention to *website analytics.*

4

UNDERSTANDING WEBSITE ANALYTICS

If you want to improve your website and help prospective patients find what they're looking for, what good is it if you don't have robust analytics on your website to understanding how it's performing and how users are interacting with your content?

Your goal with website analytics should be the continual monitoring and improvement of your website's performance. That means you need to know how well it's working in various respects: how many prospective patients visit each day, how long they stay, and which content they engage with the most. In this chapter, we'll explore some website analytics platforms and the key metrics you should be tracking to ensure your website is staying healthy.

Website Analytics Platforms

There are several analytics platforms on the market which enable you to track and measure nearly every metric known to man, but only a few dominate and are truly necessary to track your most important metrics. Two of the most popular (and useful) are Google Analytics and CrazyEgg.

Google Analytics

Google Analytics, or GA, is the most well-known analytics platform on the market. It's the grandfather of all analytics software, as it provides nearly every metric you could ever want to track. Google Analytics' features are robust, and installation of the tracking code on your website is incredibly easy. If you have a website that was designed by someone else, chances are you already have Google Analytics installed.

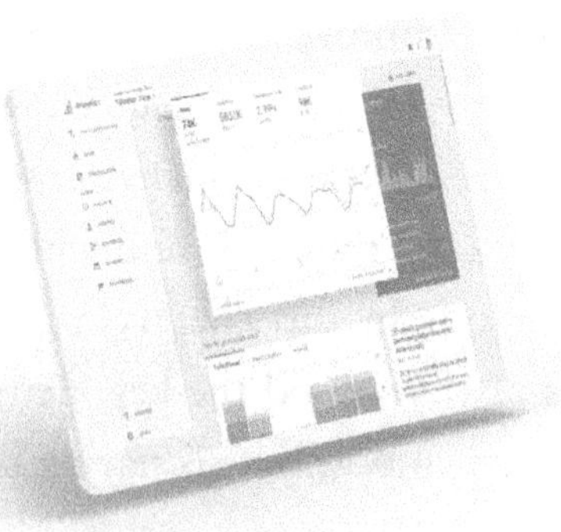

Google Analytics

Once you have the tracking code installed on your practice, Google Analytics gives you lots of tools to measure and analyze the performance of your site, including users, sessions, page load time, bounce rate, geographic area, traffic tree maps, and much, much more.

Google Analytics allows you to see what users are doing on your website in real time and compare metrics over nearly any time period imaginable. What's more, you can compare metrics from one time period across previous time periods to see how various marketing and website efforts are performing.

Google Analytics makes it incredibly easy to get started tracking your website's performance – it's the number one tool we recommend that every client use regularly to ascertain how well their website is performing. If you want to quickly add robust analytics to your website to track user behavior, Google Analytics is the perfect place to start.

Learn more at **www.analytics.google.com**

CrazyEgg

Another popular analytics platform is CrazyEgg. Although it has a unique and whimsical name, Crazy Egg is a serious software platform that provides a powerful way to know exactly how users interact with the content on your pages by creating heat maps of user activity.

With Google Analytics, you can see what users are doing on

your website – which pages they are visiting, how long they stay, which links they click, etc.

With CrazyEgg, you can know exactly where on the page users are looking, and how much attention each *visual element* of your website is receiving. Whereas Google Analytics relies primarily on statistics and numbers, CrazyEgg relies on visual displays of user activity and interest.

Example of a heat map produced by CrazyEgg

Using CrazyEgg can allow you to perform A/B tests on the placement of key website elements, including photos, videos, textual content, patient forms, and more. This is useful for organizing and laying out different pieces of page content to lead to higher conversions. Wondering where the most optimal placement of your appointment request button is on your homepage? Curious to see how changing a photo on your website influences user behavior? CrazyEgg can help you find out.

Learn more at **www.crazyegg.com**

Key Performance Indicators

There are a number of Key Performance Indicators (KPIs) to keep an eye on when it comes to your website's analytics. While the KPIs below do not comprise not an exhaustive list of all metrics you should pay attention to, they are useful in obtaining an "at a glance" look at your website's health. At a bare minimum, tracking these KPIs should give you an accurate picture of overall user behavior on your website.

Visits and Users

The *Visits* KPI is fairly self-explanatory: it's a measure of how many visits people made to your website in a given amount of time. However, many people get confused when comparing *visits* to *users* – visits is a measure of how many individual, unique visits were made to your website. This counts repeat visits as unique events. On the other hand, *users* only counts the number of real people who have visited your website. If someone comes to your website five times in a week, this will appear as five unique *visits* – but it will only count as one *user*.

Traffic Sources

Knowing how patients land on your website is just as important as knowing what they do after they arrive.

Consulting your traffic source page is a great habit to practice every time you look at your analytics data. The traffic sources page will tell you how many patients are coming to your website directly, versus being referred from social media channels, email, or search engine results. Knowing where patients are coming from is an important KPI that allows you to measure how well other marketing channels (such as social media or paid advertising) are performing, and being able to see traffic sources as a pie chart can be incredibly helpful in assessing which channels you should focus on enhancing.

Geographic Areas

Chances are your medical practice wants to target patients in your local area who can actually come in to your office for an appointment. If you run a medical practice in Chicago, you're probably not interested in attracting patients from New York or London. Of course, you can't stop patients from visiting your website (and there may be educational content on your website that is useful for people in other markets), but looking at how many visitors in your geographic region are coming to your website is an important first step to understanding how effective your website is. If you're not seeing as much traffic from your market as you might like, effective local SEO and locally-targeted ads can help boost these numbers.

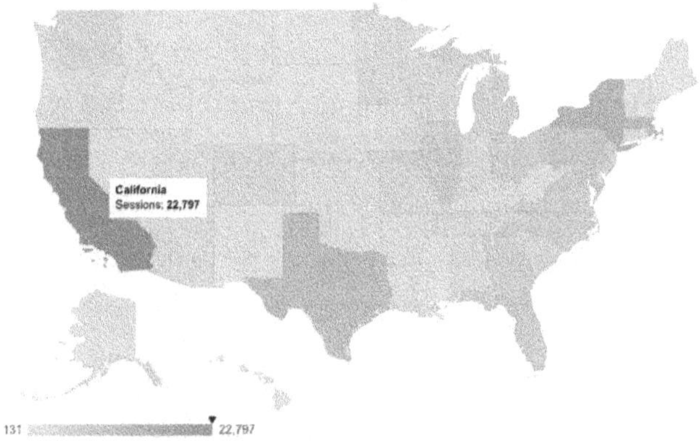

Geographic Overview in Google Analytics

Browser Technology

Another important metric to look for is browser technology. How many people are visiting your website from a Mac vs. a PC? How many view your website on a mobile device like an iPhone as opposed to a desktop? Which browsers are patients using to view your website – and does your website appear correctly on these browsers? While most websites these days can display content accurately and without error to 99% of patients out of the box, there are always idiosyncrasies between browsers and operating systems. Knowing which technologies patients are using to discover your content online is important to ensuring a good online experience for everyone.

Bounce Rate

A website's bounce rate is a measure of how many people are visiting your website and then leaving without clicking through to any other page. Bounce rate measure single-page visits, which are not very useful to your practice; thus, your goal should be to make your bounce rate as low as possible. A low bounce rate indicates that most patients are clicking through to one or more pages on your website. This means they are spending more time on your website, engaging with more of your content, and therefore have a greater chance of contacting your practice for more information or requesting an appointment as they warm up to the idea of your brand.

Traffic Tree Maps

Traffic tree maps are a visual representation of how users flow through your website. What's the typical path that a user takes when they visit your website? Which pages do they land on when they first click through to your website – and more importantly, where do they go from there? Using website traffic tree maps can help you understand which pages or pieces of content on your website are performing well, which are lagging behind or losing a user's interest, and how visitors are actually navigating your website.

Goal Conversion

If you have an desired "goals" for your patients, such as requesting an appointment, signing up for your email list, or buying a product online, using Goal Conversion in

Google Analytics can provide you clear metrics on your conversion rates and how well you are achieving those goals. Google Analytics' Goal Conversion tools can help you ascertain how many people are performing these desired actions and help you perform A/B testing in an effort to increase those conversion rates.

Two Things to Watch for in Your Website Analytics

In addition to knowing some of the most common KPIs in your analytics, it's also important to know what to keep an eye on in case your website needs adjustments along the way. While this is not an exhaustive list, below are two of the most important metrics to monitor on a regular basis to ensure your website is performing well.

Increasing Bounce Rate

Increasing bounce rate is rarely a good thing – it means that visitors are landing on your website and then leaving without ever clicking through to another page. An increasing bounce rate means that visitors are less likely to contact you, request an appointment, learn more about their medical options, or complete any goal conversions. An abnormally high bounce rate is a helpful indicator that something might be wrong with your website and is causing visitors to leave, so keeping an eye on your bounce rate over time is important. Using other tools available in Google Analytics (or a third-party tool like

Crazy Egg) can help you discover *why* potential patients may be leaving.

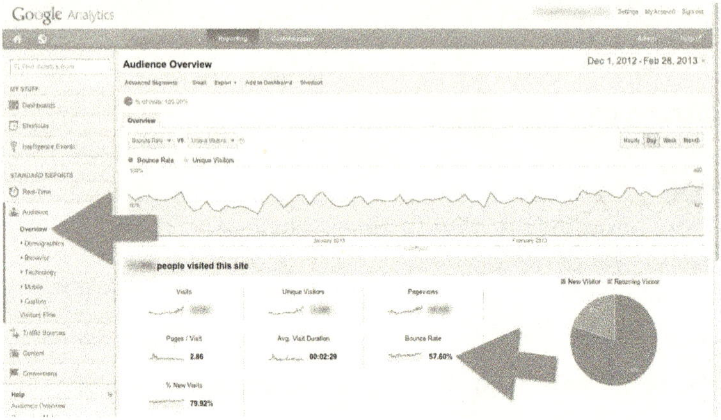

Bounce Rate in Google Analytics

Short Visit Time

A corollary to an increasing bounce rate, short visit time shows you that website visitors aren't finding what they're looking for – or perhaps that there is a usability problem with your website. Each website's average visit time is different, and it will vary depending on what people are looking for – but if you see a large drop in the amount of time people are spending on your website, this could be a cause for concern.

Using Your Analytics Data

Knowledge is power, and the more knowledge about your website analytics that you have at your disposal, the better decisions you can make with that data. Analytics data shows you what is *really* happening with your website and how users are interacting with it. Using this data to make tweaks and adjustments on a regular basis is essential to your website's health.

Have you noticed that bounce rate is increasing? Try consulting a website heat map to see what content users are most interested in. Are users exploring your website but not completing conversion goals such as requesting an appointment? Try experimenting with how you advertise and incentivize users to complete these goals. Is there a better layout you could use to feature this content?

Do potential patients rarely visit procedure information pages? Perhaps it might be time to feature your most popular procedures on your home page rather than burying them in your website's menus.

Using analytics, A/B testing, and performing small tweaks to your website on a regular basis are essential to maintaining a healthy, well-performing website. When you have the data on your side, you can make better decisions that will both serve your patients and give you a better chance of realizing your business goals. Without the data, you're fumbling around in the dark, unable to make wise, data-driven decisions that help you achieve your business goals. It's why analytics tools exist, after all.

Now that we've taken a look at basic website analytics and how website layout can influence user behavior, it's time to turn our attention to another great tactic to increase user engagement: *live chat.*

5

UTILIZING LIVE CHAT FOR MORE SATISFIED PATIENTS

Most patients have questions, and as a physician, you have answers. However, the process of asking questions can be frustrating for patients and time-consuming for your office staff: patients tend to ask the same questions over and over again, or perhaps they don't know how to phrase the question appropriately. Your FAQ section may be hard to find on your website, so you're inundated with questions from patients wondering about their condition or the services you offer.

Medical practices have every incentive to answer patients' questions in an efficient and helpful manner, but addressing patient questions and concerns can be a daunting task, especially when you get the same questions day in and day out.

Many people don't like picking up the phone, especially

Millennials and those in younger generations. For others, their questions are quick (or their needs are immediate) – factors which may not lend themselves to contacting the practice via email or waiting days for a response. Patients want answers fast – and a key part of improving patient satisfaction is getting them the answers they are looking for in aa timely manner.

If your website doesn't make it easy for patients to find answers to their questions, you're missing out on a huge opportunity to be helpful to your patients and build their trust. Utilizing robust FAQ sections can go a long way to increase the efficiency of your office staff, but there's one technology that reigns supreme over commonly-used tools like FAQ pages: live chat.

Why Live Chat?

Chances are you've encountered a website with live chat software before. The live chat window usually lives at the bottom right-hand corner of the screen, where someone may greet you and ask if you have any questions. Unlike asynchronous forms of communication like email, "contact us" forms, or support tickets, live chat enables your office staff to engage with patients in real-time.

Not only does live chat help patients get their questions answered in real time, but it makes your website a bit more friendly and engaging – all factors which serve to build patient trust over time.

So why live chat? Why not just email instead?

Well, email is a wonderful technology, but it isn't necessarily the best way to help patients get their questions answered. Emails from contact forms tend to pile up and can cost office staff lots of time replying to inquiries. Contact forms are also especially susceptible to spam and bots clogging up your inbox, and if your practice's email systems aren't set up properly, emails can easily hit spam filters. This means more work for your office staff and a longer wait time for your patients to get their questions answered.

Unlike email, both patients and practices benefit from live chat software: patients get their questions answered more quickly, and practices are able to streamline their in-office efficiency and get patients the answers they need.

The Benefits of Live Chat

Higher patient engagement

When patients visiting your website see that there's a real person "manning the phones" (so to speak), someone with whom they can chat and get questions answered in real time, they are much more likely to engage – and spend more time on the site. This doesn't mean that your live chat has to be intrusive – it shouldn't. Rather, it represents to patients that you don't treat your website like a sterile environment for marketing purposes only, but that you're interested in engaging with patients and making sure they get their questions answered and have a good experience. Most patients use live chat software to get quick responses to their questions, but it's also a great outreach tool to schedule appointments (as we'll see below). You'd be surprised how many patients will engage with a practice when the practice has live chat software that is easy for patients to use.

Opportunities to schedule appointments

You may have a patient scheduling system on your website, or you may prefer to schedule appointments only over the phone. Live chat software can give your staff yet another opportunity to either schedule an appointment directly over live chat or direct patients to your appointment request form and intake forms rather than letting patients try to find them on their own.

Patients who have filled out forms beforehand and have everything ready for their appointment lead to greater in-office efficiencies – and educating patients and providing resources via live chat software can help to facilitate that process. The end result? More patient appointments and more revenue for your practice.

Saving your office staff valuable time

Many live chat software systems offer automatic answers and "canned responses" to frequently asked questions, which can help your office staff use their time more effectively. By being able to answer the most frequently asked questions or provide patients with quick links or more information with the touch of a button, your office staff can keep engaging patients online with very minimal effort. Most FAQ pages or traditional email systems don't offer this functionality, but live chat software enables your office staff to give patients the helpful information they're looking for – all while saving time.

Automatic "away" messages

If your practice is closed or your staff is on their lunch break when someone visits your website and asks a question via chat, your live chat software can send automatic "away" messages. These let your patients know that their message has been received, but that they shouldn't expect a response right away. What's more, many live chat systems offer visitors with an option to enter their email address if your staff is away so that they can receive a follow up via email. Not only is this convenient for both your staff and your patients, but it gives your practice an opportunity to build trust by advancing the relationship to another point of contact.

Segmentation of visitors and retargeting opportunities

Not only can live chat software help you to answer patient questions, but it can also give you powerful data that you can use to customize patients' experiences on your website. Most live chat software can show you where a user is viewing your website from, what type of device they are on, and if they are coming to your website for the first time or if they are returning to pages they have visited before. This real-time data is incredibly powerful.

Additionally, some live chat software enables you to "tag" certain website visitors according to actions they have taken on your site, such as downloading a form or viewing a specific page. These insights can allow your practice to target certain visitors and offer them promotions, or otherwise customize their experience based on their behavior. Live chat helps you get more data on your side to drive better marketing decisions and deliver a better patient experience.

Customization of greetings on different pages

Most live chat softwares allow you to customize the greeting patients see depending on which page of your website they are visiting. For instance, you can ask a general question like "How may I help?" to patients browsing your homepage, while more targeted questions, such as "Do you have any questions about financing?" can apply only to those patients who are looking for financial information. If you have pages on your website dedicated to different procedures or service offerings, you can highlight the differences and ask targeted questions to enhance engagement across these pages. These features allow you to target and engage website visitors more efficiently, which saves you time and leads to a better experience for the patient.

The Best Live Chat Providers

Intercom

Intercom is one of the largest and most powerful live chat software systems out there. It offers live chat, custom greetings, away messages, email collection, and even some email marketing tools (depending on which plan you choose). Intercom has grown their product offerings significantly in the past several years to include not only live chat, but lead management, knowledge base software, and custom bots. Intercom offers easy implementation on your website and is very customizable, though it can get a little pricey depending on which features you need.

Learn more at **www.intercom.com**

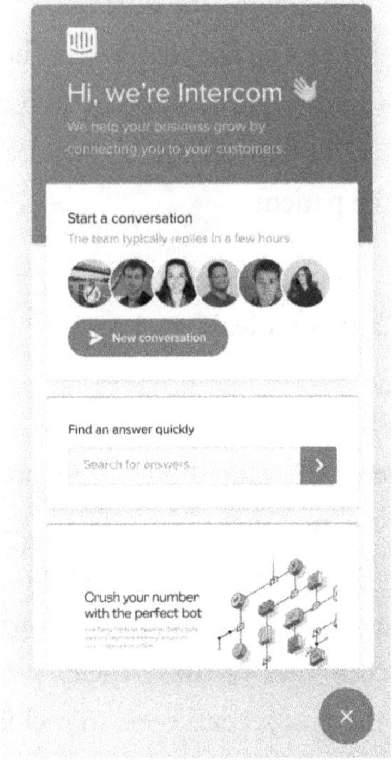

Example of an Intercom chat

Zoho SalesIQ

If you don't want to spend quite as much money on live chat software, Zoho SalesIQ is a cheaper alternative to Intercom. Zoho's feature set isn't quite as robust, and they doesn't offer any email marketing tools – only live chat and visitor scoring. However, Zoho still offers a good set of features for a reasonable price. Their software is easy to integrate into your website, so you can get up and running in no time.

Learn more at **www.zoho.com/salesiq**

Podium

Last but not least in our favorite live chat softwares is Podium. Unlike Intercom and Zoho SalesIQ, Podium offers a few tools *beyond* live chat that can be useful for medical practices, including reviews and feedback scoring. What's more, Podium allows your website visitors to chat online or take the conversation on the go with text messaging. Podium also offers ways for you to ask patients for reviews and ask them to offer feedback on your website using Net Promoter Scores (NPS) and other tactics.

Learn more at **www.podium.com**

Now that we've taken a look at why your practice should be using live chat software to engage with your patients more effectively, we'll turn our attention to another key part of your practice website to attract new patients: *content marketing.*

6

CONTENT MARKETING FOR YOUR MEDICAL PRACTICE

Why Traditional Marketing Doesn't Always Work – And What to Do Instead

Too many doctors and marketing directors think that purchasing massive email lists or scraping email addresses in plain text from websites is an effective way of finding new patients and marketing their services. Unfortunately, they're wrong. If you want to reach those who need your services most, you're going to need to adopt a new mindset.

Just like any other business, medical practices have been impacted by the changing landscape of marketing, which is pushing them to embrace new methods of connecting with patients. While email (done correctly) is an effective tool for engaging with patients, there are some other strategies that deserved your marketing director's attention. In this chapter, we'll explore one of the best ways to attract new patients to your practice: content marketing.

Content marketing is the process of sharing content such as blog posts, informational videos, photos, infographics, and more to your audience for the purpose of generating leads and attracting new patients to your practice. The best content marketing seeks to educate and form authentic connections that provide value and eventually, convert interested people into real patients.

Seek to educate at all stages of the buyer journey

If you really want your marketing to have an impact, you need really great content – and lots of it. The great news about creating content is that if it's written and researched well, it can serve you as "evergreen" content (which is content that can be re-purposed and shared multiple times via different channels, such as email newsletters, on your blog, via social media, etc). In order to be truly useful, your content has to be well-written and relevant for your audience – you can't just churn out content and hope to have an impact.

Don't be afraid to write content for multiple "buyer personas," or potential patients that may be at different stages of their journey. Some patients have already decided that they will have LASIK surgery this year and are merely looking to research providers, while others are a bit more hesitant and need more information. Writing content to educate patients at varying stages of the buyer journey is a great strategy, as it can help patients engage with you no matter where they are. We will cover these topics and more in our chapter on lead magnets and sales funnels.

No more purchasing massive email lists – utilize a newsletter instead

We mentioned that large email lists don't work – a better tactic is to create an email newsletter that you send regularly (once a week, once a month, etc) that educates patients and offers incredible value for them. While creating good content is a challenge for most medical practices, it's worth the investment. Research says you should see substantial results from these efforts – for every $1 spent on email marketing, the average return on investment is more than $43.

Email newsletters can be a great way to build stronger relationships with your patients. Never underestimate the power of connection – as we've seen, research suggests that it takes an average of seven "touch points" with a brand for us to feel connected, familiar, and comfortable with that brand. The more "connected" a potential patients feels towards your practice, the more likely they will be to choose you when they are looking for a physician…and an email newsletter is a great way to stay connected.

The Psychology of Why We Share Things Online

The Internet is inherently social. From Facebook posts and Tweet-storms to viral YouTube videos and those articles your mom keeps emailing you, we all love sharing.

But why do we share the content we discover, read, and watch online? What compels us to click that share button and spam all of our friends and co-workers with what we just found? Are we really hoping that funny cat image we found will go viral and we'll be the next (fill in the blank)? Or is sharing an act that's hard-wired into us?

To answer these questions, let's explore the psychology of why we share content online, why it matters, and how you can use these psychological principles to your advantage when marketing your practice.

WE SHARE TO PROCESS

Online sharing is having an impact on how we process and manage information. According to a 2011 New York Times Customer Insight Report, three out of four people (73%) report that they process information more deeply, thoroughly, and thoughtfully as a result of sharing it with others.

Further, more than four out of five people (85%) say that the responses they get to shared content help them to understand and process the information more thoroughly.

These numbers show that a good number of people share content to process it and get the opinions of those around them; however, different people share content for vastly different reasons:

THE 5 TYPES OF "SHARERS"

- **Altruists**: These people are primarily motivated by a sense of duty to bring valuable content to those around them, to let them know that they care. Altruists are also motivated by a desire to get the word out about causes – and brands – they believe in. While this group is less motivated by self-interest, they still likely to know that what they share was received and appreciated.
- **Careerists**: Focused on developing a strong network of personal and professional contacts, Careerists like to bring content and people together in ways that are actionable (and they enjoy getting credit for doing so). They share to create discussion and debate and to elicit useful recommendations.
- **Boomerangs**: Motivated primarily by the reaction they get back from sharing, Boomerangs like to stir the pot, start a debate and generate a lot of comments and "likes." For Boomerangs, a negative response is better than no response at all.
- **Connectors**: Sharing for Connectors is about

mutual experiences and staying connected. For Connectors, sharing is not just about distributing content, it is about including others in a shared, content-based experience. Connectors share things that will bring them together in person, such as coupons for shopping or restaurants, and they like to share to create new connections with like-minded people.

- **Selectives**: This segment shares information that they feel will be of value to a particular person, and only if they think the recipient would not have found it on her own. Given the time and consideration invested in what they share, Selectives expect that the recipient will respond and express their appreciation for the content they have found.

Not only are there different types of sharers, but there are 5 primary reasons why people share content:

1. To bring valuable, enlightening, and entertaining content into the lives of people they care about.
2. To define themselves.
3. To grow and nourish their relationships.
4. Self-fulfillment.
5. To get the word out about causes they believe in.

To share is human

When consumers encounter great content – useful, enlightening or simply entertaining – they feel an instinctive need to share it:

- Two in three (65%) report that when they find valuable information, they feel they have to share it.
- Three in five (58%) say it would be difficult to stop sharing information online.
- Indeed, the very act of learning and discovering information is inseparable from sharing it, as three in four (76%) say that sharing is half the fun of finding information.

So while technology has enabled consumers to share more content with more people more often, the compulsion to share and the enjoyment of sharing are important parts of our lives. Emotion and the nature of a piece of content can deeply influence the reasons it is shared, the way in which it is shared, and the types of people that share it. In order to make the most of your marketing by incentivizing people to share your content, consider the following principles:

Embrace connection

Appeal to customers' motivations to connect with each other – not just with your brand. Even though you're representing a business, embracing the human connection communicates a more authentic story that is more likely to resonate with your audience and get shared by them.

Trust is essential

If people don't trust your brand, they will be less likely to share your story. Don't try to con anyone into sharing your content – simply offer value and let them decide for themselves whether to share or not.

Keep it simple

The simplest, most authentic stories win. Don't try to overcomplicate things by telling too complex of a story – the best stories tell themselves.

Outsourcing Content Marketing

If you're just getting into content marketing for the first time, it can seem daunting. Most likely, your team is stretched too thin – between patient visits, administrative duties, and the pressures of running a practice, it's just hard to find the time.

Small practice? It's likely you don't have someone on staff who is dedicated to marketing (or maybe that job falls on your shoulders). And even if your practice is large enough – and lucky enough – to have a dedicated marketing specialist, giving them more duties may not be feasible.

That's why you should consider outsourced content marketing.

There are many reasons we hear from people who haven't started content marketing:

- *"I didn't fully understand what content marketing could do for us"*
- *"We were afraid of quality issues…how can we consistently produce high-quality content?"*
- *"Isn't it expensive?"*

If you've had any of those questions yourself, take a look at these stats:

- Content marketing leaders experience 7.8x more traffic than those who don't practice content marketing
- On average, content marketing costs 62% less than traditional marketing and generates about three times as many leads.

Step 1: the content marketing plan

Before you can have an effective content marketing strategy in place for your practice, you need to lay a good foundation. The first step is to produce a content marketing plan.

A good content marketing plan will begin with the end goal ("our practice wants to increase new patient visits by 20% over the next 6 months"), and will work backwards to develop stories and content that will resonate with your audience and help you reach your end goal. Your content marketing plan should detail the following things (among others):

- The service you're trying to market (for example, LASIK)
- Your target demographic and their preferences (socioeconomic status, lifestyle preferences, what social media platforms they are active on, how they spend time and money, etc)
- What types of content they tend interact with (videos, long-form content, infographics, etc)
- What categories of content you'll share (informational/educational, humorous, etc)
- How often you'll share this content with them, etc

These are just some elements of a good content marketing plan, but there are many others to consider. The more detailed your content marketing plan, the better. After all, you can't expect to build a house that stands without a good blueprint and a solid foundation.

Step 2: Research Outsourcing Options

The next step in your content marketing journey is to

consider your options for outsourcing. There are basically two ways of doing this: freelancers and agencies, and there are pros and cons to each.

Freelancers can provide a more cost-effective option, but results may vary. Many medical practices have had problems with the quality and consistency of freelancers' content. If you do find a capable and prolific freelancer to consistently produce good content for your practice, they'll likely be in high demand, so do whatever you can to keep them.

Another thing to keep in mind: for a niche industry like ophthalmology, the content needs are very specific. Anyone producing content for such a niche will need domain expertise to know what they're actually writing about, so that will be a factor to consider. This industry-specific knowledge can make finding a freelancer who is capable of producing good content even more difficult, and can mean that more effort is required on your part to do some hand-holding.

For many, hiring an agency is a more appealing option. Agencies can be more expensive than freelancers, though it's not always the case. Unlike freelancers, however, agencies can quickly scale up content production if you find messages and stories that are resonating with your audience.

And remember, content marketing costs 62% less than traditional marketing and generates about 3 times as many leads, so even if you're scaling up your spending on outsourced content marketing, you're very likely to see an increase in leads and new patient visits. It pays for itself many times over.

Worried about the quality of content you'll get? Think all of this sounds crazy? It's not. Turns out that 64% of marketers outsource their writing.

Step 3: creating systems

The system you create to manage your outsourced content marketing will vary depending on who you choose to create the content (freelancer vs. agency), what your end goal is (attract new patients, increase awareness, etc), and any number of other factors.

This is where an editorial calendar comes into play. An editorial calendar will take the goals and research outlined in your content marketing plan and put them into action by determining how often you'll push put content, how you'll share it, and how you'll fill up a pipeline with lots of content so you don't get behind.

Scheduling and automating your posting and sharing of content is another important part of creating a manageable content marketing strategy. It's not essential, but if can make your life much easier if you're able to automate as many aspects of content marketing as possible. Scheduling and automation tools are additional items that an agency can offer as part of their content marketing services.

Step 4: tracking your content's progress

Content marketing can take some time to scale up and see tangible results – but like anything in life that's worth doing, it can take time, and it's worth doing well.

This is where tracking progress comes into play. Ideally, your content marketing provider should work with you to determine the reach of the different content you've put out there – things like views, click-through-rate, social media reach, and more.

Tracking your progress is essential to determining the ROI of your content marketing investment, and if you want to see the best ROI possible, consistency is the name of the game. Even the best content marketers with the most experience will lose out to those who consistently create high-quality content.

It's simple: the practice who most consistently produces content will win. They will attract more patients and grow their businesses more than those who share content occasionally (or not at all).

Want data-driven strategies for writing better blog headlines? Check out a handy infographic at **www.messenger.md/headlines-infographic**

Now that we've explored the importance of your website, how to analyze its success in accomplishing your business goals, and how to attract and engage more patients through live chat software and robust content marketing, we turn our attention to one of the most powerful tools – and one of the least understood – in your online marketing arsenal: SEO.

PART II

GAINING VISIBILITY THROUGH SEARCH ENGINE OPTIMIZATION

7

WHY SEO MATTERS

If you have a website, you've undoubtedly heard those three magic letters a million times: SEO – Search Engine Optimization.

Understanding – and utilizing – the power of SEO is like the modern-day Holy Grail of the web. But so many people don't understand it. If you've spent any time researching how to perform SEO effectively, you've likely heard a thousand different opinions and even more "best practices," many of which likely conflict with one another.

In this chapter, we're going to unearth some of the mysteries surrounding SEO by helping you discover what it is, what it's not, what works best today, and how it relates to your practice website.

What SEO Is

Search Engine Optimization (SEO) is the process of affecting the visibility of a website or a web page in a search engine's *unpaid* results – often referred to as "natural," "organic," or "earned" results. Most SEO strategies use a combination of keywords, images, links, and social media activity to drive traffic to a certain website, all of which are designed to get the specified web page higher in search engine results.

SEO is a way of systematically presenting content so that search engines find the content that is on your website and present your content to users higher up in search results. Even more importantly than the search engine finding what content is on your website, good SEO practices place the needs of the user above the desires of the search engine.

SEO combines two major elements: your website itself, and the links across the Internet that are pointing to your website. These are collectively referred to as *On-Page* and *Off-Page SEO*, respectively. By optimizing your website and making it incredibly easy for search engines to browse and index, you are heightening your chances of Google and other search engines displaying your content when a user performs a search.

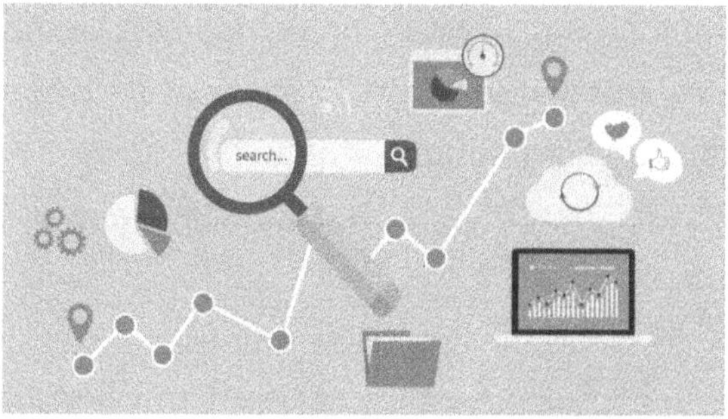

SEO is key to gaining more patients for your practice

But good SEO doesn't stop at your website. By knowing how many other websites across the Internet link to your website – and increasing this number over time – you can increase your "influence" and cause Google and other search engines to push your website higher in search engine rankings.

There's a lot that goes into On-Page and Off-Page SEO. But in order to understand how to implement good On-Page and Off-Page SEO practices into our websites, we must first examine what SEO is *not.*

What SEO is Not

There are many myths and urban legends surrounding the practice of good SEO, but very few people understand what SEO is. SEO is *not:*

- A magic bullet or a catch-all solution

- A sure-fire way to get #1 in search engine rankings
- An overnight tactic that will instantly drive more traffic to your website
- A way to "beat the system" and achieve higher success

Google and other search engines have literally spent millions of man hours and billions of dollars developing advanced algorithms that discern which content is most relevant to a user's search, and then display the best results to the user. You're not going to get around it and see overnight success with some new SEO "trick" or a "sure-fire method" that someone sold you on the Internet for five easy payments of $19.95.

How SEO Works

Let's think about search engines for a second. A search engine is not a real person, but it still has to decide what content exists on a website (this is called "crawling" a website), categorize the content and file it away, and then display that content when a user searches for something that may be related to it (for example, a phrase, the name of a business, an image search, etc).

A good On-Page SEO strategy focuses on the content. Good SEO will implement a variety of practices to ensure two things:

1. That search engines have the most opportunities possible to categorize their content; and,
2. That the website has the highest possible chance of appearing at the very top of results when a user searches for a similar topic.

Good SEO strategies place keyword-rich content on web pages, place links to other websites and other pages within their own website, utilize description tags for images and graphical elements so that search engines can understand what images are of, and so on and so forth.

Seems simple, right? Well, not so fast, because SEO changes *a lot.*

What Used to Work

In the past, the Internet saw dozens of "best SEO practices," ranging from the slightly underhanded to the downright spammy. When the term SEO was first coined, pretty much anything worked – if you could link to 1000 different websites from your own, you would be #1 on Google in no time. These spammy practices took on a variety of different forms, all of which can be categorized as "Black Hat SEO." Here are some of the most common Black Hat SEO tactics:

Keyword stuffing

Keyword stuffing was a SEO technique used by web

designers to overload keywords onto a Web page so that search engines will read the page as being relevant in a Web search.

Invisible text

Another Black Hat SEO practice was to make text "invisible" by adding white text on top of a white page in order to fit more keywords in and get a greater chance of being discovered by search engines. Users couldn't see it because it blended in with the background of the page, but search engines could read the code, pick up the text, and file it away to be displayed in search results.

Doorway Pages

A Doorway Page is a web page designed specifically for the purpose of gaining high placement in a search engine rankings. The doorway was meant to capture the attention of a search engine by containing keywords and phrases that it would pick up on. Often the doorway page would contain hidden text in order to load the page with occurrences of a specific keyword or phrase.

Adding unrelated keywords

Another practice was to add unrelated keywords to increase the likelihood that users would stumble upon a given website even when they searched for something completely unrelated.

PAGE SWAPPING

This involved changing the webpage entirely after it has been ranked by search engines, thus trying to "trick" the search engine into displaying a website with unrelated results.

These may seem like quick or easy tricks to "game the system" and achieve page one rankings (or even the coveted #1 spot), but they don't work anymore. In response to the growing number of websites that were using such methods, Google (in the interest of user experience) changed their algorithms drastically, not just to cease rewarding those sites with page one status, but to penalize the websites that utilized these tactics. It has been estimated that Google changes their search engine algorithm more than 200 times per year. Many of these changes are small tweaks in order to serve the best content to their billions of users, but some changes happen because Google is trying to combat spammy Black Hat practices like these.

Best SEO Practices Today

SEO isn't dead. There are still many best practices that can be used to form a complete and comprehensive SEO strategy and see wonderful results. These include having a responsive website that works well on mobile devices, adding keyword-rich body copy to your website, linking your social media profiles to your website (and posting to them regularly), using descriptor tags for images and other graphical elements, and linking to both external websites and other pages within your website.

At the end of the day, it's all about helping search engines understand and correctly categorize what's on your website, as well as helping users find it by providing an exceptional user experience. While search engines are not dumb, they aren't humans either, and so they need a bit of help.

But what does this mean for the physician?

Content is king

Perhaps the best advice we can give to physicians is to be regularly posting content and tweaking content on the website, most likely through a blog or "newsroom" of sorts. When it comes to modern SEO, content is king, and there's no better SEO strategy than regularly posting informational, keyword-rich content on a variety of topics to increase the chances that a search engine – or a real person – will stumble upon what you have to say.

Mobile matters

Within the last year, Google has updated their search engine algorithm again to reward those websites that are "responsive," or that work well on mobile devices. Again, this is all done in the interest of user experience, and websites that don't display legible fonts and content tailored and optimized for mobile devices will be penalized.

Know your reputation across the web

Utilizing SEO software like SEMRush can help you ascertain exactly how your website is performing across a variety of SEO metrics. No one metric is above the rest – they all work together to determine how well your practice website fares in search engine rankings. Knowing your strengths and weaknesses – as well as your website's reputation – can go a long way to improving your SEO and attracting more patients to your practice.

Sounds too good to be true? It probably is.

It's important to remember that when it comes to SEO, there aren't any magic bullets – as with most things in life, if it sounds too good to be true, it probably is. The Internet is a wonderful place, but it's full of people and companies promising that they can make you #1 on Google or increase your traffic 600% overnight...and it just isn't true. There's no way to game the system.

In the long run, good SEO strategy is an investment. It takes time to see a real return on investment on an SEO strategy...but it's all worth it. Once you have implemented a good SEO strategy, it will focus on content and both users and search engines will be rewarded by finding what they are looking for.

SEO can seem overly complicated, and if you don't live and

breathe the Internet 24/7, it's easy to get lost. But good SEO isn't really that hard to understand – it just takes a methodical, well thought-out approach, hard work, and lots of patience to see a result worth the investment.

6 Actionable Tactics for Better SEO

If you want to be #1 when someone searches for a doctor in your market, you'll need to be implementing some common SEO best practices. Here are a few actionable items to get you started:

Do your keyword research

First and foremost, keyword research is one of the most important parts of a good SEO strategy. It's estimated that 89% of patients will begin their search for a healthcare provider online before taking action…so if you want to capture those opportunities, you need to have good keywords. While keywords can seem like a simple thing, just throwing in a few words won't cut it. In order to have the best shot at being in top Google results, you'll need to do some keyword research.

Some keywords are more valuable than others – some are overused and very hard to rank for, while other keywords are hyper-specific and don't have a lot of competition. Ideally, you'll want to choose keywords that represent a mix.

Obviously "LASIK" is going to have a million results, but that doesn't mean you should exclude it as a keyword.

More specific, long-tail keywords, like "LASIK for professional athletes" are likely to be less competitive, so if that's a demographic your practice caters to, by all means include it! Using tools like Google's Keyword Planner or SEMRush to determine the competition and opportunity for your specific keywords will give you the greatest chance to pick the best keywords for your practice website and capitalize on them.

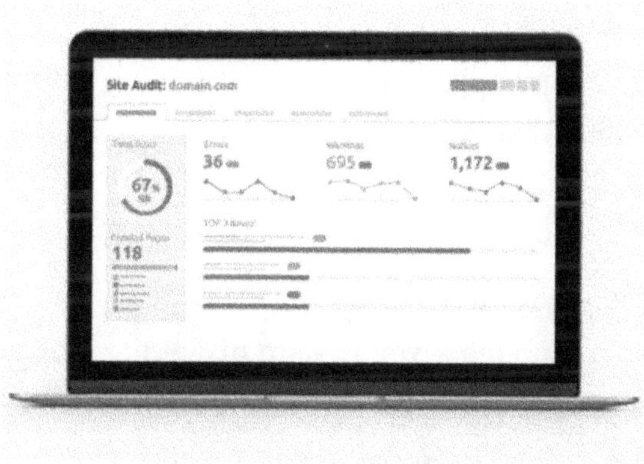

Tools like SEMRush can help you with keyword research

Make sure you have a sitemap...and make sure it's listed

Most people think of a sitemap like a website's directory, and they would be correct! The difference between sitemaps that you're used to seeing and sitemaps that rank for SEO is their format. A typical sitemap we're used to seeing or using typically has a list of all links on the website, but Google uses something called an "XML Sitemap."

An XML Sitemap is simply a computer-generated document that tells Google:

- Which pages to index
- Which pages are most important (and should be indexed first)
- How frequently content changes (giving Google a reason to check back frequently)

Many sitemaps are dynamically generated by the Content Management System your website may use. But having a sitemap isn't enough – you have to make sure Google knows where to find it! Using a tool like Google Search Console can make sure that Google knows where your sitemap is located, how frequently it changes, and which pages it should crawl. These are all important factors in getting your website to rank higher.

Prioritize content

Nothing is more attractive to Google than a site that is updated regularly, and that means content. If you don't have a blog as part of your practice website, you should strongly consider adding one. But if you do, you have to keep it fresh. Adding one blog post or news item every few months won't be enough to do it – in fact, Google sees that as a sign that it shouldn't check your website as often.

In order to get the best ROI for your efforts, create an editorial calendar with a goal of publishing at least 1-2 posts per month. Combined with some smart keyword planning, new content can not only drive more visitors to your website, but it will signal to Google that your site is active and worth checking up on more frequently. More, regular, and better content means higher search results.

Metadata matters

Metadata are the specific attributes of your website that Google uses to properly index your pages and content, namely keywords, descriptions, and alt-image tags. We've already covered keywords, but descriptions are important, too. Be sure to write a detailed description of each page's contents in a tweet-length sentence (most search engines limit descriptions to 160 characters).

It's not enough to add keywords and descriptions for just your homepage – be sure to add relevant keywords and descriptions to each page of your site, and to blog posts, too. It sounds obvious, but you'd be surprised how many practice websites we see that don't have keywords or a description at all.

ALT tags and image titles are another great piece of metadata to add on your site. Originally intended for accessibility purposes for those with visual impairments, Google and other search engines use image titles and alt-tags to index what the image is of and display the image in relevant search results.

Some Content Management Systems will automatically name images for you, but all will let you rename images yourself. Think about it – an image that's titled *55jgyad-43egsmg-9865fhsa.jpg* isn't very descriptive. Try *cataract-surgery-frequently-asked-questions.jpg* instead – Google will love you for it.

Don't neglect social media

We believe that every physician should be on social media, but it's not just so you can connect with other physicians or tweet cat GIFs (no judgment).

Having relevant social media profiles that link to your website is a great strategy for improving your SEO (plus, it gives patients another way to connect with you – what's to lose?). Having social media profiles helps Google understand that you're a real business (with real people connected to you), and it establishes links to your website on more "authoritative" websites like Facebook and Twitter.

Utilize local SEO

Local SEO is one of the most important tactics that

healthcare providers can use, because in order for patients to make use of you, they have to come in for a visit.

Not only should you add your city and the surrounding area as a keyword on your website, but make sure your practice is listed on Google My Business. Be sure to update your hours, contact information, and services to your business page, and make sure it mirrors the information on your website – this is the best way to get listed in local results.

Don't neglect other and other online profiles like Yelp, Facebook, and physician review sites like Healthgrades and Vitals – they're important for establishing online authority and will do wonders to help your practice rank for SEO (we'll explore these topics in later chapters).

Now that we have an appropriate overview of SEO in general, we'll take a deeper dive into the first of the two major pillars of Search Engine Optimization: On-Page SEO.

8

ON-PAGE SEO: OPTIMIZING YOUR WEBSITE

The first major pillar of good Search Engine Optimization is *On-Page SEO.* This refers to the practice of optimizing your website so that Google's search engine crawlers can index the content on your site appropriately and display the most relevant content to patients quickly and correctly.

According to Forrester Research, the majority of consumers (54%) find websites by typing keywords into search engines, like "ophthalmologists new york." When your website achieves high (preferably first page) search engine results, the chances prospective patients will find it and click through to your website increase dramatically.

To achieve this goal, you need to be utilizing smart On-Page SEO strategies. The challenge for web designers is that those algorithms are continually changing. For example, in 2017

Google decided to reward those websites that have a mobile-ready version, in essence "demoting" those website that did not. In this algorithm change, if the mobile version of your site doesn't work properly, your site could drop in search engine results. Staying at the top of search engine rankings requires staying on top of all available best practices, and that starts with On-Page SEO.

Why You Need to Keep Your Website Updated

Google favors websites that are frequently updated. Visitors also like to see relevant news, tips, and stories. If people see that your most recent post is from three years ago, they'll look elsewhere for the latest news.

In the old days of SEO, domain age was highly valued: the older your domain, the greater chance you'd have at ranking higher. More recently, however, Google has shifted its focus to other areas, such as the quality and relevance of content. Domain age still plays a part, but it's not as important as it used to be.

Google uses many factors when it ranks websites. "Domain authority" depends on various elements, including backlinks and page loading speed. When older websites rank better than newer ones, however, it isn't only because they have existed longer. It's because they tend to have more content, backlinks, and traffic.

What really counts today is to have a website that is "young" in appearance, features, and relevance. By this, we mean that the website is constantly updated and new content is continually added on a regular basis. This doesn't mean that you have to be continually changing the content found on your pages or blogging on a daily basis, but having new content to share at least a few times a month can do wonders for your SEO and online reputation.

Keep it visually interesting

People today like to absorb content in a variety of formats, including images and videos. It helps to mix things up and give visitors great written content along with visual stimulation. There are a variety of ways to accomplish this, including educational videos, varied imagery, and immersive visual experiences.

Nobody likes to visit websites with pages upon pages of text with nothing visually interesting to break it up. After all, our brains process images up to 400x faster than we process words, so keeping your website updated with visually-interesting content can work wonders with user retention and engagement.

The average patient will only stay on a webpage for a few seconds before deciding to move on to the next page of your website (or deciding to leave your site completely). This is why website optimization – and optimization of images, in particular – matters a great deal.

This begs the question: are your website's images getting the job done?

Imagery should load quickly

If your images are taking a while to load into a browser, it's likely because your images are not optimized for the web. Images have to be formatted before going online. Magazines and print mediums use high-quality images with corresponding large file sizes, but for the web images can be scaled down a bit. The quality still matters, but the size of the image file itself is the critical factor.

A standard high-resolution image may be 4-5MB, which will take forever to load on a web browser (even with a fast Internet connection). If you're on a mobile device, this loading time could be even longer, which will cause the majority of website visitors to abandon your site altogether. It's relatively easy to scale a 5MB image down to 200KB and still retain sharpness and reduce pixelation. These images will load nearly instantly, which is a boon for patient experience and search engine optimization alike.

Imagery needs to be tagged

Once you correctly scale, optimize, and upload the images, they need to be tagged appropriately as well. Image tagging needs to be done not only for the benefit of old browsers and accessibility best practices, to but also for search engine optimization purposes.

Images need to have "ALT tags" added to them. Alt tags are a key component of accessibility, as they simply describe the image for users with accessibility functions turned on (for instance, users who are blind).

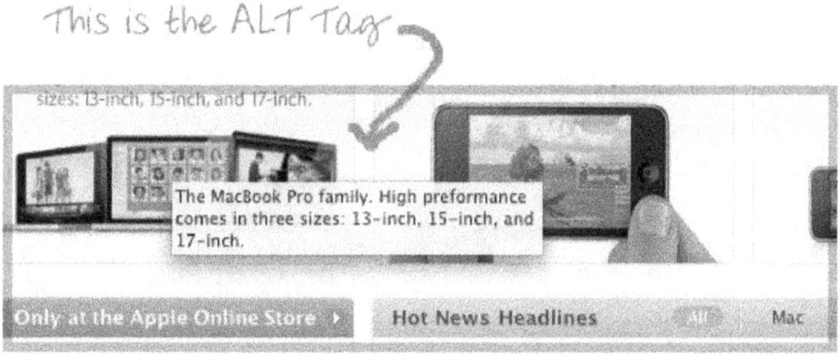

ALT tags are also important because search engines will use them to index content on a web page. Search engines like Google can't accurately "see" what's in an image (yet), so they rely on ALT tags to describe the image and index it appropriately. Having the correct ALT tags on the images throughout your practice website can be a huge benefit to your practice by helping search engines help you attract more patients.

Imagery should be authentic

Prospective patients respond to authenticity, which means the images you choose to use on your website should reflect you and your practice. If you have images like this on your website, you're doing it wrong:

If you use stock images, website visitors will notice. If they see the same image on another website and then come to your site, the message you are trying to convey becomes inauthentic and diluted: all the patient can think of is how they saw the same image on the previous site that they visited. This may give an impression that the practice wasn't thoughtful about the creation of the website, and that quality and thoughtfulness isn't important to the practice.

Trust is a huge factor for patients, and inauthentic websites can hurt business. 63% of consumers say they have engaged with disappointing brand content and 23% said they wouldn't interact that brand's content again after that. Having images that are correctly sized, tagged, and authentic will go a long way to enhancing your website's reputation in the minds of visitors and search engines alike.

Your Website's Age in Online Years

When Google ranks websites, it uses a proprietary formula that includes hundreds of factors. When you improve in any of these areas, you increase your website's value and rank better. Two websites that are in the same niche and have the same content, but were built at different times will rank differently.

To find out your website's literal age, you only need to consult your records. If you don't remember when your domain was first registered, check with your domain registrar, website hosting provider, or use a WHOIS service to look up the registration date for your domain.

At the end of the day, it doesn't matter as much how old your website is in actual days, months, or years. It's never too soon or too late to remake it in a way that's more visitor- and search engine-friendly.

The key is to provide a valuable user experience that promotes frequent and continual engagement over time. The most successful websites are responsive, updated, adaptable, and in touch with the needs of both customers *and* search engines.

If you're serious about obtaining more traffic to your practice website, it's important to show your visitors (and search engines) that you are investing in their experience and wants to provide value through new content, research, and a pleasant experience.

On-Page SEO best practices, such as updating your website, keeping images optimized, and adding appropriate keywords and metadata are all part of a good strategy, but there's another major factor that influences how Google ranks your website as well: Off-Page SEO.

9

OFF-PAGE SEO

As we mentioned before, the SEO game is always changing. In the past, it was relatively simple to throw up a website, add the appropriate code, and rank near the top. Today, SEO is not only about optimizing your website for Google to index it appropriately, but all about link building, content marketing, social media sharing, and so much more. Collectively, we refer to this as *Off-Page SEO* – activities which happen *away* from your website, but still influence how you rank for a specific keyword or topic.

Because SEO is becoming harder and harder to implement well, it's all the more important to know the right strategies that will deliver more patients to your practice. The old methods and spammy practices don't work – you need to know the right things to do. It's not about quantity of activity, but about quality.

In order to attract more patients to your practice, you need to use the right mix of SEO tools and strategies…and it all starts by defining your goals. There are two primary approaches when it comes to SEO, each of which has their merits. We like to call them the *shotgun* approach and the *sniper rifle* approach. Let's compare the benefits of each.

The shotgun approach

The *shotgun approach* to Off-Page SEO is all about ranking for as many keywords as possible. This can take a long time, but if you're willing to spend the time and money on building such an approach, it can be a powerful tool that can drive tons of traffic and revenue to your practice.

However, this approach takes a lot of time and money to get going – we're talking years and tens of thousands of dollars. This approach is also quite susceptible to Google's algorithm changes – if one keyword that you've been ranking for is suddenly dropped by Google, it can hurt business significantly.

The sniper rifle approach

That's why we like the *sniper rifle approach* to Off-Page SEO much better. Frankly, it works better for many medical practices. Using the sniper rifle approach to SEO, you should choose those keywords that are highly targeted to your audience and what they're searching for. Unlike a general keyword that could have many people searching for it, targeted keywords may have lower search volumes, but they're the right kinds of people searching for you.

Basically, you're targeting people who you know with certainty are searching for exactly what your practice offers. *We call these "long-tail" keywords.*

Put simply, it's way better to have only a few people searching for a term that you know you will rank for than to have thousands of people searching for a term that you're very unlikely to rank for. This approach also takes significant time and resources to rank for, but it's more strategic in nature – and that's why we believe it's the best choice for many practices to attract new patients with SEO.

Using the sniper rifle approach, it's also highly unlikely that a Google algorithm change will negatively affect your ranking, because you're so targeted. If you become #1 on Google with a highly specific, targeted keyword, it's unlikely that someone else is going to come along and knock you off.

Know Your Target Market

Nobody knows your market as well as you do. You know the needs, concerns, and questions that patients have when they come into your practice, and you know how to help address their questions.

Let's say you're an ophthalmologist. Maybe your practice

specializes in LASIK only, or maybe you offer every type of refractive vision-correcting surgery there is. It doesn't really matter – what *does* matter is that you've taken the time to understand exactly what your target audience is searching for and that you have a plan to capture their attention.

Starting with this awareness of your target market is a crucial step in developing your SEO strategy and building backlinks for certain keywords. Consider asking current patients how they found you. If they had to look up information online, *what did they search for?* You may be surprised at what patients tell you. This practice will help you develop ideas for long-tail keywords that you can use to drive targeted traffic to your practice website.

There are some tools you can use to aid you in your search. Google's Keyword Planner is one – although it was designed for paid advertising campaign planning, it's a great way to get additional keyword ideas and see estimated monthly search volumes and competition for said keywords. Google Trends is another great tool to explore search engine trends and interest in certain topics.

Understand Your Current Traffic

To know how to target messages to potential patients using SEO, you have to understand what current patients are doing on your site.

- Which pages are getting the most attention?
- Which blog posts are driving lots of traffic your way?
- What is getting shared the most?

Knowing these things can help you ascertain where there are opportunities to build links for keywords which will attract more patients to your practice website.

There are a number of tools online that can also help you with competitive analysis – knowing what your competitors are doing, what keywords they're trying to rank for, and what sites are linking to them. If your marketing team doesn't have the time to perform these sorts of research activities, consider hiring an agency to perform this research for you – it's an invaluable investment.

Perform an SEO Audit of Your Practice Website

Having a third-party provider audit your current SEO strategy can be a boon for your practice, as it will identify opportunities and areas of improvement both on and off your website. An SEO Audit can also help you discover which of your strategies are working and where you need to double-down. It should help you discover things like your website's search engine visibility for keywords and topics, discover where backlinking opportunities lie, and get a better picture of the competition in your market.

And even if you don't have an SEO strategy in place, an SEO audit can greatly help you discover where to get started.

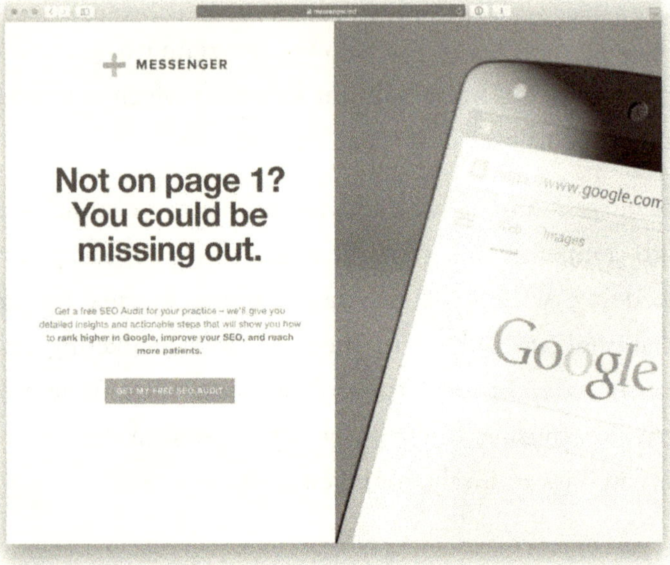

Get a free SEO Audit at www.messenger.md/free-seo-audit

Interested in a free SEO Audit for your practice? Visit **www.messenger.md/free-seo-audit**. We'll give you detailed insights and actionable steps that will show you how to rank higher in Google, improve your SEO, and reach more patients.

A Note About SEO

As with any marketing strategy, there are many things to consider when implementing SEO. As your practice gets started, here are a few things to keep in mind regarding SEO:

SEO is a Long-Term Investment

As a young kid, I used to love watch fishing shows on TV – I was always amazed at how quickly the fisherman caught his trophy fish. As I grew up, however, I learned that it's not like that in real life. Behind the scenes, the camera crew waited in the rain for hours and endured dozens (if not hundreds) of bites before they were able to get one that stuck. It took patience.

SEO is the same – while there are strategies that have much better chances of success than others, there's no replacement for time. As famed investor Warren Buffet once said, *"Even if you are very talented and make all possible efforts, some things simply take time…you can't expect to have a baby in one month by getting nine women pregnant."*

Viewing SEO as a long-term investment will produce the best results. It is only when you have correctly framed the scope and investment of such an undertaking that you will adopt the patience necessary to see the results you want.

SEO takes a lot of work

Although we've only outlined some key considerations, there are many more elements that go into a successful SEO strategy that delivers more patients to your practice. SEO takes a *lot* of work, and it isn't for the faint of heart. However, if done correctly, it can be a very lucrative strategy.

If you're going to embark on the SEO journey, plan resources accordingly, and don't underestimate how much time and effort it will take. Solid SEO can take months – even years – to develop and maintain.

SEO requires domain expertise

Backlinks. Domain Authority. Nofollow attributes. Sitemaps. Robots.txt. Long-tail keyword generation. Search engine submission. Crawl rates. These are just a few of many elements that go into a successful SEO strategy.

SEO can be very confusing if it's not a world you live and breathe 24/7. We hope this brief primer helps you understand the basics of a good SEO strategy, but if you're even somewhat lost, it's best to leave it up the experts.

Now that we've taken a brief look at how to enhance your

website's authority from beneficial SEO practice, we turn our attention two other influential tools you can use to enhance your reputation across the Internet: *Google My Business and patient reviews.*

10

YOUR ONLINE REPUTATION: GOOGLE MY BUSINESS AND PATIENT REVIEWS

When it comes to SEO, Google is king. Yes, other search engines exist, but Google represents the lions' share of search engine traffic; if you want to rank well with SEO, you have to play by their rules. The playful adage is painfully true: *the best place to hide a dead body is on page two of Google's search results.*

More and more, patients are using Google to find information about medical practices, including contact and location information. However, patients are increasingly consulting reviews that other patients have given about a practice. In fact, practice reviews on Google are becoming so influential that a healthy body of reviews can mean the difference between search engines being a major source of traffic *or almost none at all.*

It is because of this that review sites are becoming

increasingly important for doctors. Yelp is popular for restaurants and other businesses (and should not be disregarded entirely), but if you want to do well, optimizing your Google My Business information is key. In this chapter, we'll show you how to optimize your listing information and encourage patients to leave reviews that can become a boon for your practice's online reputation.

How to Win at Local SEO Using Google's Tools

Since Google is king of the SEO world, having all of your information correctly indexed with Google and their suite of tools is the first place to start with local SEO. Utilizing Google My Business is a no-brainer to give your practice the best chance to rank competitively for key search terms, but surprisingly, so many medical practices never bother to ensure their Google My Business profile is accurate or offers value to their patients. If you don't want to be like most practices, the tips below should help set you apart.

Make sure your information is correct

There's nothing worse than Googling a business only to find out that they have moved locations or have inaccurate information on their profile. Ensuring your practice information is up-to-date is the first step in utilizing the powerful tools Google My Business offers. This is especially important if you have more than one practice location. Not only that, but many online business directories will "scrape"

Google My Business listings to populate their own databases, so if your information is incorrect or out-of-date on Google, patients looking for information elsewhere will suffer as a result.

Use your Google My Business profile to answer questions and provide updates

Google My Business allows patients to ask questions about the business. Not every patient will click through to your website's contact form to ask a question – many will stop right at Google My Business. Because of this, answering patient questions on Google in a timely manner is key to maintaining a good online reputation. What's more, these patient questions are publicly available and can be useful to other patients, so in that sense, your Google My Business profile can become a "crowdsourced" FAQ of sorts.

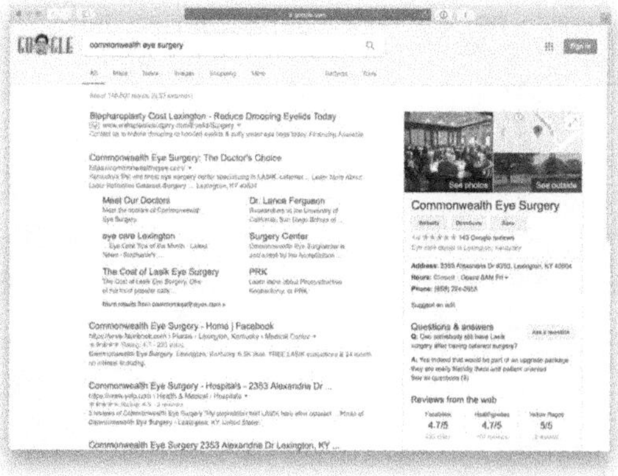

Google My Business Listing for Commonwealth Eye Surgery

Review your analytics

Unlike many other review sites, Google My Business gives you monthly updates of how your photos, statuses, and answers to questions are performing – you can see how many people are viewing your photos, clicking through to your website, asking questions, clicking on contact information, and the like. Because a Google My Business listing is the first thing many patients will see when searching online for your practice, knowing how many patients are engaging with your Google My Business information is key to assessing patient interest and getting a high-level view of your overall online reputation.

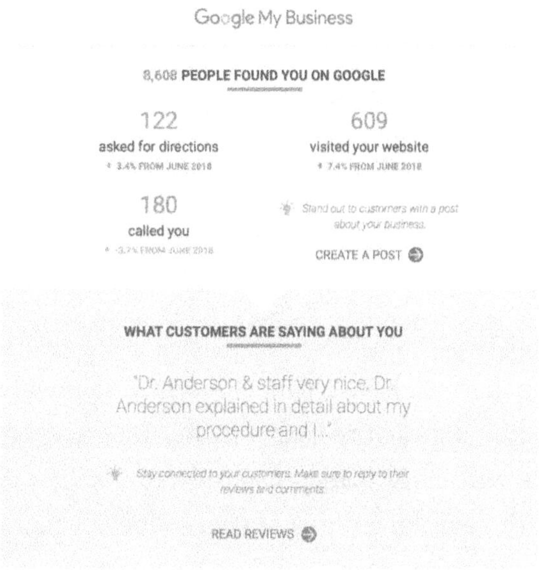

Example of Google My Business monthly analytics email

Manage patient reviews

Perhaps the most important of Google My Business is its review feature. Not only should you encourage patients to post reviews of their experience at your practice, but actively engaging with patients on Google My Business' review section demonstrates to other patients that your practice is engaged and interested in providing a good experience. Below, we'll examine why patient reviews matter, and how to make the most of them to benefit your practice.

Why Patient Reviews Matter

There are many review sites where patients can leave honest feedback and opinions about their experience at your practice. Google My Business is perhaps most popular due to the search engine's ubiquity, but others like Yelp, Healthgrades, and Zocdoc offer opportunities to enhance your practice's reputation around the Internet.

Ensuring that you have accurate information on all of these platforms is a great first step to take. Internally, you may want to encourage patients to leave a review of their experience by making it part of your follow-up routine.

Quantity of reviews isn't a joke for bottom-line revenues. According to data from Zocdoc, the 25% of doctors with the *most* patient reviews received *five times more appointments* than the 25% with the fewest. In other words, physicians with more ratings are far more appealing to patients.

Of course, quality of service and the star rating given to practices matters, too. By driving up a practice's overall rating by one half of one star (for instance, from 3.5 stars to 4 stars), Zocdoc found that the average doctor will increase their number of monthly appointments by 37%.

How to Get More Patient Reviews

If you want to get more reviews to bolster the reputation of your practice online, there are several ways to do so, each of which we'll explore here.

Want more reviews? Just ask!

There's no harm in asking patients to consider leaving a review after their experience is over, but you have to deal with any and all feedback they give. If they had to wait a long time in your office or experienced anything that was less than optical, they could leave negative feedback. Keep this in mind when asking patients for reviews.

When asking previous patients for reviews, place an emphasis on the fact that you want them to be honest. Patients should never feel pressured to write a glowing review of your practice – they should feel respected and free to write an honest review of their experience. If you communicate to patients that you really desire to improve – not merely get a 5-star review online – patients will be more likely to offer their feedback and give you positive reviews. It shows humility and a willingness to make the experience as good as it can be for everyone else. Explaining to patients why reviews are such an important part of your business goes a long way.

Make collecting reviews part of your routine

Not only can you can ask previous patients for reviews of their experience, but you can incentivize current patients to write reviews of your practice as part of your internal procedures. This can be done in person, over a follow-up email sequence, or with marketing collateral such as business cards with a link to write a review, small brochures, or flyers.

Eye Center of New York, one of our clients, has done an excellent job at this. As part of their follow-up process with each patient, they encourage patients to fill out a brief experience survey (which is only used for internal feedback). If patients respond positively, the system then encourages them to write an honest review of their experience online. As a result, the Eye Center of New York has over one hundred 5-star reviews featured on their website and across popular review sites such as Google, Yelp, Healthgrades, and more. It is a powerful example of social proof that has helped grow the practice and attract more patients.

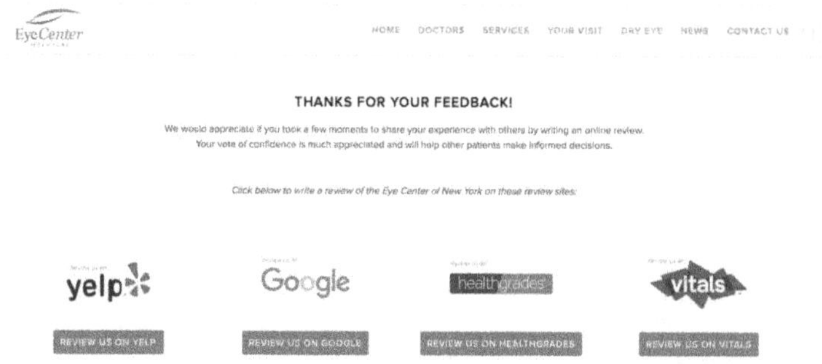

Eye Center of New York has an excellent system for encouraging patient reviews

How to Deal with Negative Reviews

Sometimes, patients are dissatisfied with their experience. Whether it's a result of poor service, an "off" day, or a patient who seems determined to have a negative experience despite your best efforts, bad reviews happen. Knowing how to deal with them effectively is the key to showing other patients that you deeply care about patient experience, regardless of what the naysayers proclaim.

The first step to take with any negative review? *Apologize.* Practicing empathy and seeking to understand where the patient is coming from is not just damage control – it's an honest attempt to collect feedback, improve, and ensure that future patients have a better experience.

However, apologizing alone won't get the job done. Addressing patients' concerns about their experience goes a long way, too. Demonstrating to your patients that you are interested in making things right not only alleviates their concerns, but it shows to other patients reading reviews that you deeply care about the experience and satisfaction of *every* patient, not just the ones who write good reviews.

Not every negative review is a deal-breaker that cannot be rectified. Sometimes, a simple miscommunication has taken place, and occasionally patients will amend or update their reviews when a doctor reaches out, shows empathy, and seeks understanding among all parties. Again, seeking to understand and make things right – in whatever way you are able – will go a long way.

Importantly, never argue with a dissatisfied patient. If you come across as argumentative, it will not only solidify their opposition to your practice, but it gives them a megaphone to project their dissatisfaction to everyone.

As you can see, patient reviews matter. They are a strong signal of social proof that can immensely help – or hurt – your practice. If you want your reputation to thrive both online and off, focusing on patient reviews is key.

But while reviews are important to bottom-line revenues, there are other important drivers of success in this area, too. Aside from reviews, how can you attract more patients to your website? And once they are there, how can you incentivize them to engage and offer their information in exchange for some valuable information you provide?

In the next chapter, we'll explore one of the most powerful tools you can use to build trust among prospective patients and ultimately get more appointments: the lead magnet.

PART III

ENGAGING PATIENTS EVERYWHERE ON THE INTERNET

11

BUILDING A PATIENT LEADS PIPELINE WITH LEAD MAGNETS

If you want your medical practice to thrive, you need to be continually filling your pipeline with new leads. Patient leads are the key to growing any practice, but they're not always easy to get. For some specialists, such as ophthalmologists, this can be achieved through referral networks of other physicians who don't perform the specialized procedures; however, for other doctors, co-management may not be the most effective strategy.

Another effective way of getting patient leads is word of mouth referrals from former patients, but it's not the only way. Word of mouth referrals from satisfied patients go a long way and are incredibly important to your overall reputation among patients, but if you want to create a robust pipeline of patient leads, you should use a mix of tools and tactics to diversify your leads.

If you want to harness the power of the Internet to your advantage, you'll need to implement digital tools to help attract new leads. In this chapter, we'll look at some of the best strategies for doing so, including one that stands above the rest: the lead magnet.

What is a Lead Magnet?

A "lead magnet" is an offer that provides patients with free information in exchange for a small piece of information – usually their first name and their email address. Lead magnets answer questions that patients have or assist them in their research about a certain medical procedure, a condition, or comparisons between two similar product offerings. Here are some examples of content that could be turned into lead magnets for a physician:

- Free Report – LASIK or PRK: Which is Right for Me?
- Free Download – 5 Questions to Ask Your Child's Pediatrician
- Checklist – The Best Daily Supplements to Improve Joint Health
- Free Guide – How to Know When It's Time for Your Parent to Have Cataract Surgery

Lead magnets can take on a variety of forms, including free

guides, checklists, blog posts, resource lists, downloads, "locked" content, etc. The key is to offer your patients *incredible value that they can immediately act upon.* Patients understand that by submitting their information, they will be placed on an email list and will hear from you again, and for the value they are receiving, this is an acceptable exchange.

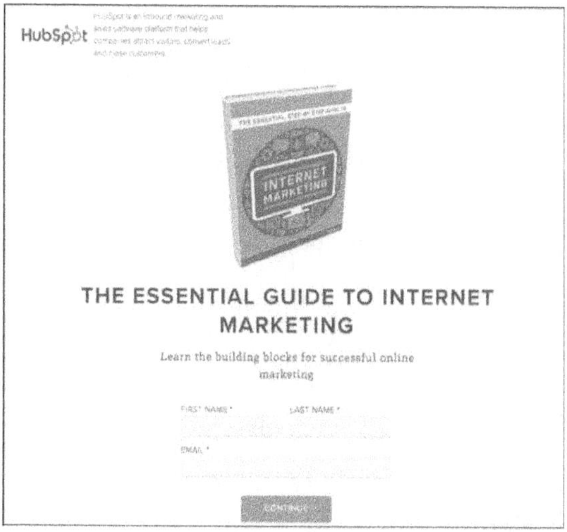

Example of a lead magnet from Hubspot

Part of the value of a lead magnet is that it automatically sorts out qualified leads from everyone else. Although it takes only a few seconds and a small bit of information, these are just enough to prevent patients who aren't really interested in your services from downloading such an offer. As a result, you know that the patients who *do* engage with your lead magnets are interested and can be placed in the "middle of the funnel" (more on this later).

Why Are Lead Magnets Important?

Lead magnets are a crucial part of an online marketing strategy because they obtain information from your patients with their consent. The act of downloading a lead magnet offer establishes a relationship that can be carried on over time with the information the practice now has about the patient.

The goal here is not to be spammy or to annoy patients with emails all the time; rather, you want to use emails to educate your patients, offer them more value, and build a relationship that can hopefully be converted into revenue farther down the road. In some instances, patients who respond to a lead magnet offer may give a practice multiple opportunities to convert them into revenue by becoming a "repeat customer" or referring friends to the practice because of the great experience they've had. Unlike cold email or paid advertising, lead magnets engage with patients who are almost certainly interested in what you're offering; as a result, the opportunity to turn these visitors into paying patients is much higher than with other forms of lead generation.

But Isn't Email Dead?

If you follow digital marketing at all, you've probably heard people proclaim the "death" of email. And yet, email continues to serve as *the* core communication platform of our digital lives. Between 2014 and 2018, the number of email accounts in existence worldwide is expected to grow from 4.11 billion to 5.23 billion. *More than 100 billion emails are sent and received every day of the year.*

What's more, email has an incredible ROI. A recent survey from the Digital Marketers Association found that email generates an average of $43 in revenue for every $1 spent by a business. Email isn't just comprised of spammy practices and unsolicited messages, either: 72% of U.S. consumers said that email is their favorite way of communicating with companies with which they do business.

Our inboxes may be filling up rapidly, but email is far from dead. The vast majority of consumers *want* to receive email from businesses they care about, *so long as the email is relevant and the business is providing value.*

There's a huge opportunity out there for physicians to utilize email in a powerful and effective way. All you have to do is craft the right strategy and provide value...and that starts with understanding where your patients are in the sales funnel.

The Almighty Sales Funnel

You've probably heard the term "sales funnel" before. But what is it? A sales funnel is a process that prospective patients (or any consumer, for that matter) progresses through as they make the journey from doing research to becoming a devoted customer.

There are three main stages of the sales funnel: research (which is what we call *top of funnel*), interest (*middle of funnel*), and buying intent (*bottom of funnel*). Some marketers may use different terms to describe various stages of the funnel, but in general, a sales or marketing funnel is divided into these three categories.

As we've seen, it takes several "touch points" with your brand to get patients to trust you and become interested in what you offer (research indicates that seven is the magic number), so repeated exposure to your offers is key. By crafting a smart sales funnel and understanding which stage each patient is in, you can craft messages targeted directly at them; relevant messages and repeated exposure build trust and help convert potential patients into revenue for your practice.

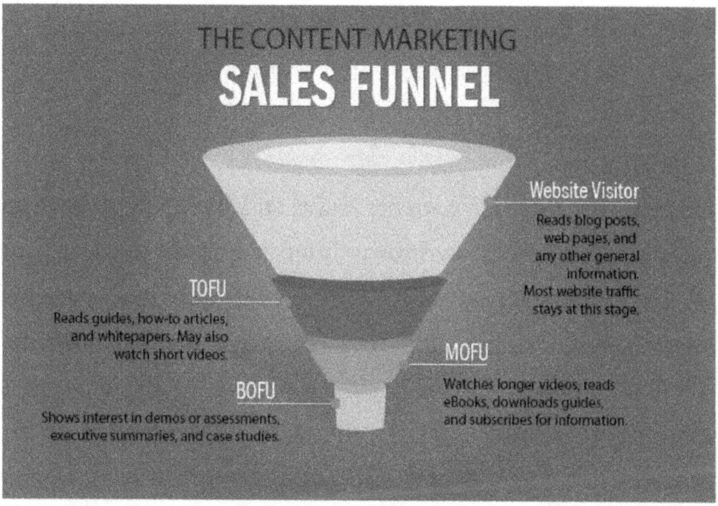

Example of a Sales Funnel

Top of Funnel (TOF)

When patients are in the Top of Funnel stage, they're just poking around. They may be researching different providers or trying to answer a question about a medical condition or procedure. First impressions among TOF patients is key. You have to get off on the right foot and begin building trust from the outset if you want to convert these potential patients into revenue farther down the road. This is where good website design, coupled with a lead magnet that answers the question they're researching will put you ahead of your competitors. The goal with TOF patients is to read their mind and offer a lead magnet that makes them think, "Oh my gosh, that's *exactly* what I've been looking for!" If you can do this, you're well on your way to converting them into a real patient – and revenue for your practice.

Middle of Funnel (MOF)

Middle of Funnel patients have taken a step beyond research and have shown some interest in your practice, but they may not yet be fully committed yet. These patients have likely clicked around to a few pages on your website, filled out a contact form, or even downloaded a lead magnet that demonstrates interest in a certain condition or procedure. MOF patients still need some nurturing – you haven't gotten an appointment request yet – but they're more interested than the Average Joe who lands on your website, stays for a minute, and then goes back to scrolling Facebook. Providing value to these patients is key – use your lead magnets to offer incredible amounts of information and value to them. Do whatever it takes to get these patients to the Bottom of Funnel, because that's where the revenue lies.

Bottom of Funnel (BOF)

When patients reach the Bottom of Funnel stage, you know that they both qualify for a certain procedure and have demonstrated clear intent that they are researching *you* to help them with their medical condition. BOF patients may have filled out an online self-test to help determine their options for treatment (you guessed it – this is another lead magnet), or perhaps they have already scheduled an appointment for an initial visit. Bottom of Funnel is where the money is – these patients have trusted you enough to take the next step and meet you in person. The relationship is quite solid at this stage, but the journey is far from over – now you must focus on the in-person experience and deliver value to them at every step of the process.

How to Craft an Effective Lead Magnet

When it comes to crafting an effective lead magnet for your practice's lead generation efforts, there are a few things to keep in mind. Obviously, you want to offer incredible value to your patients – value that is commensurate with the value of the personal information they give you (their name and email address). Once you establish exactly what your lead magnet will be (say, a free report on the differences between LASIK and PRK), there are two things you will want to do:

SELECT AN EMAIL MARKETING PROVIDER

If you don't already have an email marketing provider to deliver email newsletters or other forms of email marketing, now's the time to get one. A good email marketing provider will be able to segment lists of subscribers based on their actions, and (most importantly), will be able to deliver email sequences in an automated manner. It's important to note that this service will *not* be the same as your regular email *service* provider (such as G Suite by Google) – email marketing providers are unique and serve a distinct purpose apart from everyday email. If you're stuck researching an EMP, some of our favorite email marketing providers are MailChimp and ActiveCampaign. A quick Google search should also yield good results.

Set up your email automation campaign

You should have a different automation sequence for each lead magnet you utilize. An automation sequence is your opportunity to tailor the message to each patient depending on which lead magnet they downloaded on your website. It's your chance to form a relationship, offer value, and build trust – before your new patient even walks in the door!

For instance, the first email you send your new lead will contain the offer itself (the thing they signed up to download). It may also contain a question about their situation, such as "Why are you interested in LASIK?" Keep in mind HIPAA rules when communicating with potential patients, and always avoid giving medical advice or asking about specific conditions over email. Keep the questions general and lighthearted – the goal here is to *start* a conversation and begin nurturing the relationship.

Subsequent emails can ask other questions, offer more resources depending on a patient's response to previous emails, or even suggest that they take a self-test or request an appointment. By "dripping" these emails out over a few days, you can form and deepen a relationship with patients over time, so that when they walk in the door to your practice, they are already "primed," know what to expect, and are more likely to have a good experience.

A key benefit of using an email automation sequence is that it takes *zero* time for your practice to maintain – it's a "set it and forget it" system. As long as you are driving traffic to these lead magnets and offering incredible value with the magnets you place on your site, the patients will slowly trickle in. If you build up your library of resources and lead magnets over time, the number of patients you will attract will slowly grow until you have a robust pipeline of patient leads.

Utilizing Multiple Lead Magnets

The most effective practices we've seen utilize a mix of different lead magnets to cater to different audiences, as well as patients who are researching different topics. As always, understanding where your patient is in the sales funnel is key.

You're not limited to just *one* lead magnet to offer prospective patients value – the sky is the limit! Try to think of as many resources as you can that will provide patients with value as they research providers and their options. If you can create a resource that will assist a patient in their journey whatsoever, *you absolutely should* – more often than not, patients will gladly exchange their email address for the knowledge you have to provide.

For example, you can have different lead magnets targeting different procedures, different geographies, or for different demographics or types of patients. You can place these lead magnets around your website of course, but you can also create ad campaigns that advertise individual lead magnets in an attempt to start a relationship with a patient.

Now that we've examined lead generation tools that take place on your website, we turn our attention to a great way to connect with patients and build your audience *outside* of your website: social media. It's ubiquitous in our society, but unfortunately many physicians don't know how to effectively use social media to enhance the online reputation of their practice and connect with new patients elsewhere on the web – so it's time for us to get social.

12

SOCIAL MEDIA FOR THE PHYSICIAN

The Biggest Lie About Social Media

Let's face it: social media has much of the medical world confused. At first glance it might seem like an embarrassing thing to admit, but it's really not. So many physicians have personal profiles on popular social media sites like Facebook and Twitter, but they still haven't yet found a way to integrate these channels into their practice and clinical work.

So what's the biggest lie about social media? *That it doesn't matter.*

For some reason, doctors have been tricked into thinking that social media doesn't matter for their practice. This could be because they've seen others try it and fail. It could be because of the ever-present fear of HIPAA compliance. It could be that they don't understand how much time needs to go into running a successful social media channel, or they may not know where to start.

Whatever the reason, it's a huge lie that social media doesn't matter for the medical industry...and it's one we want to fight. Social media is useful for doctors for a number of reasons. Here are a three of the most important ones:

Social media expands your reach and can help draw new patients in.

Google and other big search engines often highlight profiles from social media websites like Facebook and Twitter above regular websites, so having active social media channels is a great way to expand your reach online beyond just your website. Also, having links to your social media channels on your website and vice versa (cross-linking) is a boon to your SEO, which increases the chances that your website or social media profile – or both – will be discovered.

Social media helps engage with potential patients.

Sure, it may seem like many patients may not interact with their doctor online – and the vast majority may not. But don't fret, some still do! Especially if your website may not be as visible, social media channels are a great way for potential patients to get in touch, book an appointment, or learn more about your practice.

SOCIAL MEDIA IS A GREAT TOOL FOR COMMUNICATING WITH OTHER PHYSICIANS AND STAYING UP-TO-DATE WITH INDUSTRY NEWS AND EVENTS.

From our experience, this is the element of social media that doctors tend to understand the most. Though patients may use social media to discover and engage with you or your practice, this is the primary reason physicians should be on social media. Following other physicians in your area and around the world can be a wonderful way to discover new talent, stay up-to-date with industry happenings, and promote collaboration among physicians.

Social media may not be for everyone, but it's an absolute lie that it doesn't matter. It is only when physicians try their hand at social media tools that they can discover how much these platforms really matter for discovering, connecting, and collaborating online.

Messenger Ophthalmic Marketing @messengerMD · 17 Feb 2016
Did you know that one third of consumers now use #socialmedia sites for #health-related activities? #hcsm
5
65
149

One third of consumers now use social media for health-related activities

5 Common Myths about Social Media

Let's face it: social media as a tool for business is here to stay. Whether you choose to utilize Facebook, Twitter, LinkedIn, or any other number of platforms, the opportunity that social media affords physicians to connect and engage with patients is astounding.

But many doctors are wary of using social media as a tool and taking advantage of all it has to offer. Below are some common myths that people believe about social media, and our responses to them.

MYTH #1: SOCIAL MEDIA IS JUST FOR MILLENNIALS

Yes, social media may be incredibly popular among millennials (those aged 18-34), but it's not just a tool for them. In fact, while the 25-34 age group is most popular on Facebook, (accounting for 29.7% of their user base), older generations are beginning to use social media platforms more and more.

While millennials are certainly "digital natives" (as many would be hard-pressed to remember a time before the Internet and digital tools), older generations (the "digital immigrants," if you will) are embracing social tools as a part of their everyday lives.

Myth #2: social media has no return on investment

Myth #2 is all about investment, specifically that social media has no return on investment. In reality, however, the opposite is quite frequently the case. Social media has quite a high return on investment...you just have to know what you're measuring.

When it comes to ROI on social media, many users get confused, thinking that follower count, the number of "likes" on your page, or how many retweets you got last week are the prime metrics. However, these are what the startup community has coined "vanity metrics" – they may feel good, but don't really mean anything.

The important thing to remember about social media is reach – and reach means return on investment, though sometimes it's hard to see.

Just because you didn't get as many retweets last week as you would have liked to doesn't mean that your efforts were useless. How long did it take to compose that tweet? Maybe 30 seconds? Go and look at your Twitter insights, and you'll probably see that through favorites, retweets, and mentions, you had a reach of several thousand people (or more, depending on your following)

Whether you're spending dollars on social media advertising or just going after organic reach, it's important to remember that even if one new patient visits your practice or one new doctor follows you and likes what you have to say, that's return on investment. Is it a large new contract, hundreds of new patients visiting your practice, or publication in a peer-reviewed journal? No…but it is increasing your reach, and that matters more than you can know.

Myth #3: nobody turns to social media when it comes to their health

Myth #3 is the belief that nobody turns to social media when it comes to their health, so it's useless for doctors to have a presence there. While one could argue the finer points of what audience each social network is intended for, we'll let the stats do the talking here:

- 18 to 24 year olds are more than 2x as likely than 45 to 54 year olds to use social media for health-related discussions.

- 31% of health care professionals use social media for professional networking.
- 41% of people said social media would affect their choice of a specific doctor, hospital, or medical facility.
- 60% of doctors say social media improves the quality of care delivered to patients.
- More than 40% of consumers say information they find via social media plays a role in how they deal with their health.
- 60% percent of social media users say they trust social media posts by doctors over any other group.
- One in five Americans use social media websites as a source of health care information, according to National Research Corporation's Ticker survey, the largest, most up-to-date poll on consumer health care opinions and behaviors.
- One third of consumers now use social media sites for health-related activities.
- 73% of consumers would welcome social media-based tools like make an appointment, or ask a question.

Myth #4: social media is a waste of time

This myth harkens back to the return on investment myth by asserting that social media is a waste of time. At

Messenger, we believe that social media can be an incredible asset...but it all depends on how you use it.

If you're turning to social media to scroll through an endless news feed full of GIFs and cat videos, then yes, social media is likely to be a waste of time for you, and dilutive to your practice. But, if you have carefully and thoughtfully crafted the right message, the right following, and offer and engage with useful information that educates, inspires, and establishes yourself as a thought leader in the field, social media is anything but a waste of time.

Time on social media must be spent with a purpose in mind. This is what most people today forget – social media has become a distraction, an escape, something to do with your phone when you're waiting for the next thing in your day and don't want to appear bored (its' ok to admit it – we do it too from time to time).

But time spent on social media purposefully can be one of the greatest assets your practice has. It boosts engagement, establishes you as a thought leader, helps connect and educate, and can ultimately lead to more website or in-person visits. When the connections are as plentiful as they are on social media, the possibilities are endless.

Myth #5: I don't have anything to say

Our fifth and final myth is one many of us have experienced: why turn to the Internet when I don't have anything to say? The prospect of not having anything to say is a daunting one, especially when it takes time and investment to grow (and maintain) a following on social media.

The fact is, you *do* have something to say.

But what is it? What will I post? What if I run out of ideas? And what if I have an idea but nobody likes what I have to say? It doesn't matter – just start saying things. It's literally the only way to develop your voice. You may feel like you don't have anything to say, but that's not true. You just haven't found your voice yet.

For starters, begin with what you know. If you specialize in a particular area of medicine, start educating people about it. Offer information and provide value, inspire and connect with followers, and make social media a valuable resource for those that follow you (they'll love you for it).

Over time, your voice will develop. You'll begin to discover what you like posting, what you like reading and seeing, who you engage with most, and how you can tailor social media to make it the best resource possible – both for you and your followers.

The Do's and Don'ts of Social Media for Doctors

Social media is an incredibly powerful tool, but when it comes to utilizing it in the medical field, certain rules apply.

Here are some best practices for successfully using social media as a doctor:

DO BE ON MULTIPLE PLATFORMS.

Different audiences are on different platforms, so having active profiles on the most popular ones (Facebook, Twitter, LinkedIn, Medium, and others) offers opportunities to reach more people and post different kinds of content.

DO ENGAGE WITH PATIENTS – MAKE IT ABOUT THEM!

It's a harsh truth of social media: nobody cares about you - people care about themselves. Especially as a physician, not many people will follow you or engage with your brand if you make it all about you. Engage with patients, offer questions, and post amusing or inspiring things, but don't just make it about you!

DO EDUCATE AND OFFER VALUE.

Patients and industry players will be more likely to follow and engage with you on social media when you offer value through education and interesting content. Because their visits are infrequent, patients are unlikely to follow physicians on social media...unless you make it worth their while. Posting interesting stories, photos, facts, and news can increase the chances of new people engaging with your practice online.

DO REMAIN ACTIVE AND POST OFTEN.

Nothing is worse than a business's social media profile that hasn't been utilized in three years (or three months, for that matter). If you're going to be on social media (which you should), it requires commitment - you need to post often (daily for Twitter, weekly for a blog, at least weekly for Facebook, etc) and get people interested in what you have to say. Dormant accounts don't do any good, so keep up with it!

DO MAKE IT ABUNDANTLY CLEAR THAT ANYTHING OFFERED ON SOCIAL MEDIA IS NOT MEDICAL ADVICE.

A disclaimer is an important part of a social media profile for any physician. Make it clear to followers that tweets, postings, and other content offered online is not medical advice, and encourage patients to come in for a visit if they are looking for medical attention.

DO NOT POST MEDICAL ADVICE.

I'm guessing that you don't want to get in trouble for violating HIPAA regulations, so the best idea is to never post medical advice online. Education is good, but nothing can replace a face-to-face interaction between a medical professional and a patient, and social media isn't likely going to be an avenue for accurate diagnosis anytime soon. Save yourself the headache of potential HIPAA violations and don't offer advice online.

DO NOT Over-Post

While active engagement on social media is certainly a good thing, it's important to not over-post. There are some unwritten rules of the road for posting on social media, including how frequently to post. The general guidelines are to tweet up to 3 times/day, post on Facebook 2 times/day (7 days a week), and on LinkedIn up to 3 times/week, but only on weekdays.

How physicians can effectively utilize social media

It seems that almost everybody these days has a profile on some social media website, but there is much debate on whether or not healthcare professionals should have a professional presence on social media. While social media is certainly is not for every physician, here are a few tips that can help the savvy doctor utilize social media to grow their online presence.

Be on the most popular platforms

There are more and more social media platforms popping up each and every day, but for physicians to get the most out of social media, it is important to be on the most popular (and most relevant) platforms. For most doctors, this will mean having a presence on Facebook, Twitter, and LinkedIn, though some physicians with interesting images to share may see benefit from being on Pinterest. Google+ is another option, though you likely won't see as much engagement.

Link your social media to your website...and vice versa

In the world of social media, verification is key. Your patients want to know that you are who you say you are, so it's crucial to link your social media accounts to your website, and vice versa. Doing so helps build credibility and maximize each and every touchpoint - a patient may stumble upon your Facebook account and end up visiting your website as a result, or vice versa!

Linking your social media to your website may also help with SEO to your website, as Google tends to give better search rankings to social media accounts, and having more links to and from each account will push you higher up in search results.

Engage with patients

Sure, some patients will follow you for news and updates, interesting facts, and the like, but at the heart of every follow on social media is the desire to connect and engage. When new patients like your page on Facebook or follow you on Twitter, engage with them and say thank you! A little personal touch goes a long way, and with each genuine engagement, your followers will build a stronger connection with your brand.

Provide value and educate – don't just ask for engagement

For physicians, social media is an incredibly useful tool to educate, inspire, and offer value. The most important thing to remember when using social media is that your fans and followers on social media aren't interested in you...they're thinking about themselves.

Any opportunity you have to offer value, whether that means posting interesting facts, inspirational stories or testimonials, or awe-inspiring photos that have to do with your practice is a huge opportunity - and one that too many physicians miss out on.

Keeping your fans and followers' interests ahead of your own by offering value at every turn is the way to build a strong presence on social media, and ultimately, a stronger brand.

Post different types of content on different platforms and encourage patients to connect in multiple ways

Each social media platform is tailored to provide a different type of content: Facebook is for longer stories and videos, Twitter is for short updates and photos, and LinkedIn is for professional updates and news items. By tailoring your content to these different platforms, three things are accomplished: 1) your followers get what they expect from each form of social media, 2) patients are encouraged to follow you on multiple channels, and 3) you multiply your opportunities to connect with new patients (because not everyone is on every social media platform).

What to Post

"I'm a doctor, but I'm a little lost on how to use the Internet to the advantage of my practice. What types of content should I post online to get the most out of the investment I've made in my website and social media?"

If you've ever asked yourself (or anyone else) this question, rest assured that you're not alone. We get it all the time – and it's not just from doctors. If you're a little lost when it comes to what you should post on your website, blog, or social media channels, here are some ideas for starters:

Educational content

- About different diseases and conditions
- About different procedures to treat these diseases
- Common misconceptions people have about surgery (and more importantly, what's true about them)
- Common misconceptions people have about the medical profession or your speciality

Behind the scenes content

- Biographical content about you and the other physicians in your practice
- Fun facts about your office staff
- Behind the scenes in your office
- "Out of the Office" content - remind your patients that you're a normal person just like them!

Promotional content

- A promotional video, if you have one
- Quick, helpful links to your website
- Promotions, discounts, and offers your practice may be running
- Online trivia and polls on Twitter

Sharing others' content

It's also important to remember to share others' content, not just to post your own. Sharing content from a variety of sources is a valuable tactic to increase engagement among your followers and the original author and their followers.

A few more tips for posting content online:

- Share a variety of content. We've all seen the Twitter accounts that have "automated" their posts...and only post the same photo OVER AND OVER AND OVER AGAIN. Don't be like them - spice it up! Try to choose a mix of different types of content to engage with patients in different ways.

- Remember your audience. If you're going to be targeting other physicians with your posts, a little more technical content is ok…but if your primary audience is potential patients who are interested in your services, keep the content you post accessible for everyone.
- Use a service like Buffer to make your life easier. Buffer uses analytics to select the optimal times to post your content for the best changes of higher engagement. You can connect multiple social media accounts and schedule tweets, posts, and the like so that you can post on your own terms and don't have to constantly be checking social media.
- Above all else, focus on providing value. The most engaged followers and the best business- leads will only come from social media if you are constantly offering value at every turn…and asking for very little in return. The time will come when you can ask your followers for something in return (like subscribing to your newsletter or clicking on a link to your website), but don't get caught up in that – just focus on providing value.

When Is the Best Time to Post on Social Media?

Hopefully you now recognize the power of social media to grow your brand, spread your message, and attract new patients to your practice. But social media marketing for doctors can be hard. It's not enough to just create content and post it whenever it "feels right" - some times are better than others.

So what's the best time to post on social media?

Unfortunately, there's no perfect answer. Patients browse different platforms at different times (and for different reasons). Good post timing depends on the platform you're using, the message you want to send, how your target audience uses the platform to engage with brands like yours, and other marketing goals.

Social Media for Physicians: 4 Strategies to Attract New Patients

The first thing doctors need to know about social media is that it's not *just* social. The fact is that the majority of users on Facebook, LinkedIn and Twitter go to those sites to find information about businesses and the products and services they offer. For example, 73% of the 1.13 billion active daily users of Facebook go there "for professional purposes," and 63% of Twitter users say they use that platform to find news and events outside of the social arena.

Marketers for businesses as diverse as manufacturing, software as a service (SaaS), consulting — and medical — are increasingly embracing social media to grow their companies. For example, 66% of marketers in a recent survey from Hubspot saw a substantial increase in leads for their businesses by spending as little as 6 hours a week on social media, and 90% say using social media has increased exposure and visibility for their businesses.

The question, then, is not whether using social media can grow a business, but rather how best to do it.

How one pediatrician found new patients on social media

When pediatrician Dr. Natasha Burgert launched a Facebook page and Twitter account, her intention was simply to share relevant health information to help the existing patients in her Kansas City, Missouri practice. She quickly learned that her social media posts provided an ancillary benefit: new patients.

Today, posting blogs on subjects like HPV prevention and the role of vaccinations, Dr. Burgert has garnered some 8,000 Twitter followers and more than 1,400 "likes" for her practice's Facebook page. As she explains:

"I use social media to share health information. My goal is help our kids in Kansas City make good health decisions. As a consequence to that, I think that patients and families in our community are very interested in what we do here, and we certainly get new patients to our practice because of our social media efforts."

How You Can Attract New Patients with Social Media

Although every practice is different, there are some common sense rules of engagement which will help all medical practices attract new patients. Here are 4 strategies to attract new patients for your practice:

Have clearly articulated goals

You have to begin by deciding what you want to achieve with social media. Do you want to attract new patients, or is your goal strictly educational? If you do want to target patients, who are you going after? Is your sweet spot the LASIK market, or are cataract and refractive surgeries your bread and butter? Your goals will dictate the kinds of content you post and the nature of any calls to action within those posts.

Keep your content current and relevant

You need to assume a patient-centric point of view in the content you post. What are your current patients' major concerns and questions? If you don't know, you should take the time to ask them, and post blogs on those topics on social media.

You can also use social media tools, like Facebook's Audience Insights to identify the most frequently asked questions by any target audience. You can answer those questions to establish authority, and provide links to your website.

Finally, it's a good idea to stay on top of the latest developments in your field by scanning press releases from professional organizations and other industry publications if you don't already.

Keep your posts positive and professional

Don't make the mistake of being overly colloquial or chummy – prospective patients want to have confidence in your abilities. There's nothing wrong with being occasionally lighthearted, but in general, you should maintain a professional tone and a relentlessly positive attitude.

Seeking to educate patients and provide tremendous value is the name of the game. It's ok if you do so in an informal manner (nobody likes a boring person), but remember, you have your professional reputation to think about, and patients are placing extreme trust in you as their surgeon… so make sure your practice's social media stays positive and professional, just like you.

Be responsive

Visitors to social media sites use those platforms to initiate conversations. That means the content you post will generate questions and, at times, complaints. In fact, nearly *72% of patients who complain on Twitter expect a response from the company within an hour!*

Be sure to visit your social media pages daily. When patients or prospective patients ask questions, answer them, quickly, succinctly and authoritatively. When they complain, take their concerns seriously and address them professionally.

Social media offers the opportunity to find and influence those new patients as you demonstrate your competence and authority. By articulating your key goals, educating with relevant content and being responsive to questions and concerns, you can build trust in your abilities and gain immeasurably in new and loyal patients.

5 Social Media Best Practices to Help Your Medical Practice Grow

Let's be honest: it's easy to get caught up on social media. We've all done it at some time. All you want to do is post an update…but then you notice you have messages! Ooh, a notification! Oh look, someone shared something interesting!

Suddenly, an hour has passed and you're wondering where the time went.

If you don't want to get caught up in the time-wasting

tendencies of social media but do want to get the best ROI for your investment and grow your practice by using social media, we've got a few best practices for you.

Prioritize.

In order to make social media an effective tool for you and your practice, you have to know not only how to spend your time, but where to spend it. Facebook and Twitter are usually the best social media platforms for doctors to connect with patients and other industry influencers alike.

Prioritizing doesn't just mean choosing where to spend your time – you have to know what you're going to say on each platform. Posting content that isn't consistent with your practice values and message can significantly detract from your brand. Remember, your social media profiles are just as much a part of your brand as your website is – so maintain a consistent message and prioritize your message for each audience you're trying to reach.

Plan ahead and schedule

No business has ever become successful flying by the seat of their pants. If you want to grow, you'll need to have a plan in place to achieve the growth you want to see. That doesn't mean things will always go according to plan, but without a growth plan, you won't be able to measure the results your strategies are achieving. Just as you would set marketing goals for your practice, you should set goals for social media engagement as well.

As important as planning is planning ahead. As it pertains to social media, taking advantage of post scheduling tools like Buffer can be an incredibly helpful way to manage your time and get the biggest bang for your buck.

Actively engage

Obtaining a positive ROI from social media doesn't happen by being like the Wizard of Oz, hiding behind the curtain. To get the best results, you need to engage with your audiences on each platform.

Don't just wait for messages or comments – don't be afraid to get active in conversations that pertain to your practice by answering questions from potential patients, responding to users' comments (both praise and criticism), and posting relevant content that will help patients discover your practice and earn you those valuable "follows."

Consistently engage

There's nothing worse than coming across a business's social media page and realizing that it hasn't been utilized in 3 years. In fact, this is the #1 reason why social media proves to be a hindrance for businesses instead of a boon.

Humans are creatures of habit, and to some degree, we like consistency and regularity. Don't overdo it, but don't be afraid to engage with users and post frequently and consistently.

Consistency isn't just about posting regularly – it's also about posting the right types of content (this goes back to best practice #1 above). Don't post content that's off-brand or seemingly random – if you don't have anything to say that really adds value to your fans' timelines, don't say anything at all.

Analyze your results

In order for social media to be an effective tool, you've got to know how users are responding to what you post. Utilizing the analytics tools social media platforms provide is a good way to understand your audience better, including what they like, what content hasn't performed well, and ways to improve and tailor your message to your audience.

If you advertise on social media, you have even more powerful tools at your fingertips, because the social media giants want to prove that ROI to you. Find out which ads are ignored and which ones are on fire. Know which days of the week are most popular for your content. Do a deep dive on what content interests your audience most. Then, take all of this information and transform your content into exactly what will generate traffic, interest and activity.

At the end of the day, social media is just one small part of an effective online presence for your medical practice. As we've seen throughout this book, there are many elements of crafting an effective online strategy that attracts new patients: a well-designed website, content marketing, social media, lead magnets, effective patient communication, SEO, and much, much more.

Engaging in each of these elements of effective online marketing takes significant time and investment; however, thoughtfully investing in each of these areas should help you grow your practice and deliver more positive patient experiences for years to come.

AFTERWORD

Putting It Into Practice: How to Use What You've Learned

Patient choice is on the rise, and at the end of the day, patient experience is often times the determining factor in how well a medical practice thrives in our new economy. Digital marketing done well (all with the end goal of a terrific patient experience in mind) is a key element to a practice's success. Get your digital marketing and patient experience right and the results will follow.

We hope this book has been helpful and has given you some ideas and pointers on how to make your digital marketing as effective as it can be. However, we understand that this much information can be overwhelming, and if you're not familiar with the nuances of digital marketing, it can be quite confusing. That's why we've created a companion guide to help.

Your 90-Day Digital Marketing Action Plan

To help further distill this knowledge into actionable steps you can take to improve your digital marketing, we have created a **90-Day Digital Marketing Action Plan** that will help you take what you've learned and apply it to your medical practice. You may want to go through the Action Plan yourself, or you may want to hand it off to the person responsible for your website and marketing at your practice. Regardless of *who* does the work, we hope that it is helpful in your quest to take your website and digital marketing – and ultimately, your patient experience – to the next level.

To access the Action Plan,
visit **www.messenger.md/action-plan**

For individualized recommendations on how your practice can improve in its digital marketing, contact us at
www.messenger.md/contact

WHAT CLIENTS SAY ABOUT MESSENGER

"We reached out to Messenger when we had very little capacity to redesign our website. As more folks got involved on the project, the team at Messenger provided great leadership, valuing the opinions of others while urgently shepherding the project along. They were very adaptable and had wonderful ideas to help us along to get to a drastically improved web presence in a short amount of time. I would highly recommend their team and look forward to working with them on future projects."

– David Franco

VP of Commercial Operations, Visiometrics

"Messenger has been a tremendous partner in developing and maintaining our website. From layout and design to hosting and updating, they have been and continue to be competent, responsive, and professional at every step along the way."

— Daniel Chang, MD

Founder and Medical Director, Empire Eye and Laser Center

"We were very pleased with the high level of service and professionalism provided by Messenger in developing our new website. They demonstrated great attention to detail and excellent response to our needs with good solutions provided and wonderful creativity. It was a very efficient and effective experience for our company and we highly recommend their services."

— Joe Wakil, MD
FGH BioTech

"It was a pleasure working with Messenger to capture our video testimonials. We weren't able to be present for the video shoot, but they were very responsive and informative during the whole process – I felt confident that we were in good hands. Plus, our experts were grateful for the professionalism and guidance their team offered once they were in front of the camera. Thank you!"

— Stefanie Henning
Director of Marketing, Paragon BioTeck

"Messenger designed a new website for us, beautifully incorporating our message and targeting it to our specific customer groups. The speed with which pages were built and features were added was excellent. Almost every change we wanted made was addressed *the same day!* We could not be happier with the end product and are looking forward to continuing to work with Messenger to maintain it."

— Noam Rosenthal

Product Manager, Visiometrics

"...hands-down one of the best professional interactions I've had. I would highly recommend Messenger to any potential client."

— Gary Wörtz, MD

Chief Medical Officer, Omega Ophthalmics

Cataract & Refractive Surgeon, Commonwealth Eye Surgery

LET'S CHAT

We at Messenger are incredibly proud to have worked with some of the nation's leading physicians and medical technology companies to help refine their brands and grow their practices through online marketing – a*nd we're always looking to develop great long-term relationships with new clients.*

If you need help with any element of your practice marketing, please don't hesitate to reach out! We would love to work with you.

For individualized recommendations on how your practice can improve in its digital marketing, contact us at

www.messenger.md/contact

www.ingramcontent.com/pod-product-compliance
Lightning Source LLC
LaVergne TN
LVHW041211050326
832903LV00021B/569